Letters t

CW00481924

Letters to a
Sex Therapist

Intimate Answers to Ticklish Questions

Sandra Alexander

'But we're so well suited to each other . . . !'

Horizon Books

Cartoons by Colonel Mustard

Dedicated to Lena Lakomy

© 1988 by Sandra Alexander.

First published in 1988 by Horizon Books Ltd,
Harper & Row House, Estover Road, Plymouth PL6 7PZ, United
Kingdom. Tel: Plymouth (0752) 705251. Fax: (0752) 777603.
Telex: 45635.

British Library Cataloguing in Publication Data
Alexander, Sandra, 1946-
    Letters to a sex therapist.
    1. Sex relations
    I. Title
    306.7
    ISBN 1-85461-000-7

Typeset by Peregrine Typesetting, Perranporth, Cornwall.

Printed and bound in Great Britain
The Guernsey Press Co. Ltd., Guernsey, Channel Islands.

Preface

This book has been compiled from letters and answers, displayed in my 'Personal Problems' column on PRESTEL. The column can be found every week on World Viewdata Services – PRESTEL no. 546030. For those not in the know, PRESTEL is British Telecom's national public videotex service, described by one as 'a miracle of modern science'. I am a sex therapist, described by another as 'the first automated agony aunt'. There you have it, in a nutshell.

I do my best to respond to all readers' genuine problems relating to sexual and emotional issues. My responses tend to be succint due to the format of PRESTEL.

May I thank everyone for writing to me and reassure all concerned that nobody's identity is ever revealed.

I'm not intending to titillate when I state that some of my advice is necessarily sexually explicit – merely to stress that this book is not reading material for the faint-hearted.

I would like to acknowledge the following people for their inspiration/ support and sometimes both:

Debbe Alexander, Margaret Ballard, Penelope Cave, Cliff Chapman, Susan Davies, Maureen and the Miller Girls, Uncle Sly's Band, Elizabeth Stanley, Harvey Tish, Anne Wort, my builders, butchers, car mechanic, dentist, greengrocers, newsagent and all associates on the street where I live.

I would like to express special appreciation to my friend and colleague, José von Bühler for his perspicacious perspective and to Christine Shone, local heroine and wizardess of the word processor.

Finally, a big hip-hip-hurrah for the apples of my eyes, Liz and Tash. But next time I write a book, could I please have a little less background music?!

Sandra Alexander

Contents

1

Sexual Problems From Men

It's a funny ol' life. Take yesterday as one example. A chance encounter in the checkout queue at Safeways with a bloke I know I know but can't place. Suddenly it hits me. He black belt. Me red. Didn't recognise him in karateless mufti ... but back to the issue in question.

The word has spread and, somehow or other, he knows that I'm a member of the newest profession. The conversation goes like this:

HE: Your job must be interesting.

ME: Can be.

HE: Actually, I was wondering if I could have a word with you.

ME: Do.

HE: The problem is that I can only thrust intra-vaginally eight times before ejaculating. I won't be happy 'til I reach my goal.

Who told him to count his thrusts, I wonder, as I pay for my dog food? It's yet again the false idea that sex ought to follow a pattern ... that there's a right and wrong way of doing it. Not so. In the endeavour to become sexually laid-back, one must always remember the golden rules ... it's different strokes for different folk; shifting thrusts for shifting lusts!

★

I love my girlfriend very much but am worried that I'm not good enough as a lover. It's got to the point that I feel very anxious when we have sex. Do you have any advice?

Much of the anxiety that men experience in sex is related to trying too hard to please or impress their partner. I get the feeling that this might be your problem. It also sounds as if you are trying to pretend that the anxiety doesn't exist and want to push on, come what may. Not a good idea for, if you force yourself to have sex when you are in this state, it's bound to lead to difficulties. Much better to sit back and share your feelings with your girlfriend. For all you know, she could be perfectly happy with your lovemaking and will be able to reassure you that you are worrying unduly.

★

I am a 20 year old male and was a virgin until three months ago when I met my girlfriend who is much older than me. I quite like her. The problem is that, when we have sex, I can't seem to come although I don't have this problem when I masturbate. Please help because it is depressing.

Sounds like you are suffering from a condition known in the trade as retarded ejaculation. Men who have this problem usually feel desire and get their erections easily enough but are unable to 'let go' and allow an orgasm to happen. Now, while we Sex Therapists do have our methods of making you come, I must say that I am more concerned about your relationship with this woman. You tell me that you 'quite like her'. Hardly enthusiastic. What does this mean? Write to me again but, this time around, tell me how you feel about your girlfriend. Let's look at your emotions rather than your ejaculatory reflex.

★

My wife loves making oral love to me. I always wash myself before she does this. Do you know a suitable deodorant I could use in addition to this?

Deodorants are not terribly tasty and could turn your wife off oral sex rather than turn her on even more. You are obviously paying attention to hygiene. Why do you want to use a deodorant? I presume that your wife is having a good time and is happy with your normal genital odour. As Alex Comfort says in *The Joy of Sex* – 'nobody wants peach sauce on, say, scampi!'

★

I read something in the papers about the drug papaverine. It's the drug that you inject into the penis to get an erection. The report says these injections are dangerous. What do you think?

Papaverine is a drug which, if injected into the penis, can cause an erection lasting for up to four hours. In this country, it's used as a treatment for both premature ejaculation and impotence. While the use of papaverine has had a certain amount of success, side effects are not uncommon. What goes up doesn't always come down and I have heard of doctors being called out in the middle of a particularly good game of golf, in order to deflate a persistent and painful erection. Don't think, for one moment, that technological solutions to sexual problems hold no interest for me. But I do feel that they should be considered as a last resort and would be far happier recommending some form of talking therapy in the first instance.

★

I've been married for five years. We have an excellent sex life most of the time but, sometimes, I ejaculate too quickly. My wife doesn't mind but I do. If you could offer an expert opinion, I would be grateful.

My expert opinion is that you should not create problems when they don't exist. If you are having an excellent sex life for most of the time, then you are doing very nicely thank you. Your wife is obviously contented. Why aren't you? Perhaps you are comparing yourself with the unrealistic male figures presented to us in erotic literature. Maybe you are anticipating mutual, earth-shattering orgasms every time – again, totally unrealistic. Listen, if I were in your shoes, I'd count my blessings and enjoy ejaculating as and when it comes!

★

I have been trying to get my girlfriend to perform fellatio. She is not keen on the idea. I believe that semen prevents tooth decay. If this is true, how can I convince her that she would benefit from the act?

Semen preventing tooth decay is news to me. A possible line of dental research perhaps, but I'm not quite sure how one would go about setting up control experiments! As for your problem with your girlfriend, if she's not keen on the idea of fellatio, I'd leave the subject alone for the time being. People's sexual tastes do tend to change and you may well find that, as your sexual relationship progresses, your girlfriend may be willing to try out new ways of expanding your sexual repertoire.

I am 37 and, during my adult years, I have only had one girlfriend and that wasn't until I was 32. This is because I find it very difficult to make the first move. I feel that I have some kind of block in my mind and am afraid that I will be refused by the woman. During my relationship with my girlfriend I was unable to reach a climax whilst love-making and I felt inadequate and unable to please my partner. I would appreciate any advice or comment that you could give me.

You are not alone in experiencing the problems that you describe. Many men are shy of women – some, even petrified. There are also many men who occasionally don't reach a climax. Ejaculation and orgasm depend very much upon the circumstances of love-making and, contrary to popular belief, do not have to occur during every sexual experience.

It seems to me that you are suffering from what Sex Therapists call 'performance anxiety'. You need to learn how to relax and simply enjoy what's happening. You need to develop the ability to discuss your anxieties and express your preferences to a partner. It's not your job to run the whole sexual show – it would probably help if you and a future girlfriend were to share the active and passive sexual roles.

Think about seeing a therapist and working on some of these issues. In therapy, you'll also be able to look at your low self-esteem which seems to extend to other aspects of your life and not just to your sexuality.

★

What is the 'squeeze technique'?

The 'squeeze technique' is an exercise which some Sex Therapists prescribe as a treatment for premature ejaculation. It has a good success rate, providing that you know what you are doing and squeeze in the right place at the right time!

Basically, the chap who wants to delay ejaculation, has to recognise 'the point of ejaculatory inevitability'. That's the point at which, even if the roof caved in, he would not be able to prevent himself from ejaculating. It's just before this stage that the squeezing has to start. The squeezer will find that her man loses pre-ejaculatory sensation if she exerts pressure on his penis in a particular way. For specific details, contact one of my colleagues.

★

Mine is an embarrassing problem which I hope you can help with. Recently my girlfriend bought me a pair of skimpy swimming trunks which are lovely. The only trouble is that, every time I put them on, I get an erection which I can't get rid of. The more I try not to think about it, the worse it gets and the more embarrassed I become. I find that normally I get an erection very easily from the slightest little thing. Am I oversexed or do a lot of fellas 'suffer' from this problem?

It's quite common to get an erection when wearing tight fitting trunks. Are you oversexed? I don't know. I'm not quite sure what the phrase means. But I do know that, if you were genuinely embarrassed about your 'problem' – you could solve it very easily. Try fifty lengths of the swimming pool, for starters!

★

I recently wrote to you about whether there was any danger in having anal sex with my girlfriend. Since my last letter we have tried this and both enjoyed the experience. Are we breaking the law? Are there any dangers involved? Do you think we are a strange couple?

Whilst anal intercourse between heterosexuals is illegal in this country, it's a practice which many couples try out occasionally. So, no, I don't think that you are a strange couple in wanting to experiment in this way. But there are dangers involved.

Anal intercourse may cause injury and extreme gentleness on the male's part is essential. It may lead to troublesome infections if mixed with straight vaginal penetration. And, for people at risk of contracting the AIDS virus, I ought also to mention that anal sex falls into the highest risk category.

★

I have just read Shirley Conran's book Lace *in which someone puts a goldfish up a woman's vagina. Do you think I ought to try it out on my wife?*

Don't be so absurd. Goldfish up vaginas may well sell novels but, in real life, please stick to what nature intended!

★

My girlfriend likes me to 'go down on her'. Privately, I think it's terrible and also a health risk. What should I do?

Let's say that you were going out to dinner; you fancy an Indian meal and your girlfriend is dead set on Chinese. You would, I hope, discuss each other's needs and reach a compromise. Likewise with sex. People's differing sexual preferences must be respected if a relationship is going to work. Communicate your needs to your girlfriend and listen to hers, too. If you care about each other, you'll sort it out.

As for oral sex being a health risk... well, it's less of a risk than conventional vaginal sex without a condom. Nowadays, my friend, sex is a health risk for many, so keep informed and take appropriate precautions.

★

My problem is that every girl I sleep with wants to marry me after the event. I can't understand this and it is destroying my confidence. I just want to have fun and this threat of heavy relationships is gradually impeding my performance. I don't think I'm that great a lover so what am I doing wrong?

Dear oh dear... you do seem a little on the selfish side if you don't mind me saying so. Your confidence is being threatened because everyone wants to marry you. Listen, my friend, I reckon that the music has stopped and it's time to jump off the sexual merry-go-round. It doesn't appear to suit you any longer. What's more, if you fail to change direction you are bound to contract and pass on some sexually transmitted nasties en route. Surely there are ways of having fun which don't involve leaving a trail of lovesick women behind you? How about a stint of voluntary work at your local geriatric hospital?

★

Over the last few years of an otherwise happy marriage which has produced three children, my wife's interest in sex has become reduced and unpredictable. We have discussed things at great length. She has seen her doctor and a marriage guidance counsellor but to no avail. We are now driven to distraction and it is affecting the rest of our lives. We feel we would benefit from some professional help but Sex Therapists are not listed in the yellow pages!

I hope you didn't encourage your wife to go to her GP and visit a counsellor on her own. When a couple has sexual problems it's often more productive if they are able to seek help together.

See your GP for referral to a Sex Therapist or write to the Association of Sexual and Marital Therapists, for details of NHS and private therapists in your area. Good luck!

★

What is a happy hat? Is it something to do with sex? My mate told me I ought to buy one and try it out on my wife.

A happy hat is an appliance which fits on to the end of the penis and is supposed to provide clitoral stimulation for the woman. I must say that I am extremely wary of such contraptions which, more often than not, drop off the penis and get lost inside the vagina. If your wife is complaining that she doesn't get sufficient clitoral stimulation, try using your fingers, toes, tongue or whatever. I doubt that a happy hat is the answer to a maiden's prayers!

★

I have a very sexually active relationship but wish to have a family later on in life. I have heard that the male sexual organs only produce a certain amount of sperm in a lifetime and I am worried that I may have already used up my quota. Please put my mind at rest and tell me if this is true as I can't stop thinking about it.

It is a total myth that each man has a limited supply of sperm. The testicles, as well as producing the male hormones, continue to produce literally millions and millions of sperm which are released every time ejaculation occurs. So you can relax and continue to enjoy yourself. There is no reason to believe that you should not be able to have a family later on.

I was always obsessed with my own sexual pleasure but, since I stopped reading Playboy *and switched to* Cosmopolitan, *I've gone the other way. I just want to satisfy my wife and, if she doesn't have a terrific time every time, I get very miserable. Please advise.*

Sacrificing your macho feats for the benefit of womankind is not an easy act to follow. Perhaps you should stop reading all magazines for a month or two and concentrate on finding a more balanced way of being for yourself. If you intend to ignore your own needs totally in order to focus exclusively on those of your wife, you are doomed to failure. Sex is not just about giving as it's not just about taking. Pleasure each other and give some thought to the team spirit. You can't play every single shot alone in a game of mixed doubles.

★

My wife and I are concerned. We cuddle a lot but only want to have sex about once a month. We are both 30 and we are both extremely busy with our careers. We don't normally meet up until about 10 pm every evening and that is presumably part of the problem. I think we both put a lot of energy into our work and sex doesn't seem too important at the moment. But I have friends who talk about doing it five times a night. Do you think there is something wrong with us?

No, I don't think there is anything wrong with you. If you are both putting vast amounts of energy into your careers and spending little time together, it's not surprising that you are not making love five times a night, is it? It's all a question of choice, really. As long as you and your wife are both content with your present lifestyle, then you have no reason to be concerned. If you are not happy with the status quo, you'll have to work out whether you can or are prepared to modify your working lives in order to make extra space for emotional/sexual needs. If you need them!

Why, I wonder, are your friends boasting about their sexploits? But that's another problem...

★

I have suddenly developed a fear that I might die during sexual intercourse. I am a 33 year old happily married man, fit and healthy but this fear is ruining my sex life. Help!

The chances of you dying during sexual intercourse are extremely remote. I can't quote you any recent statistics but, some years ago, the Japanese studied this very subject (quite how they went about their research, I can't imagine) and found that death during sexual activity accounted for only 0.6% of all sudden deaths. Furthermore, when death did occur it was more likely to happen during extra-marital encounters.

There's a very clear message in this little tale. Providing you don't go in for sexual scenarios with strange women in Japanese hotel rooms, you should be okay. Have I reassured you?

★

My wife and I consummated our marriage on our wedding night. We've been married for three months but I still cannot find her clitoris. Please advise.

The clitoris, the small knob of tissue at the front of the vulva, is the seat of female sexual excitement and certainly worth finding. I would suggest that you treat yourself to a copy of *The She Complete Guide to Sex and Loving* by Doc David Delvin and pay particular attention to the chapter entitled 'A Conducted Tour of the Sexual and Erogenous Zones'. Study the diagrams of the female genitals; then study the real thing. I'm sure you'll find what you're looking for!

★

Have you any advice to give to a man who is bored out of his mind with safer sex?

If you care about your health, my friend, then safer sex precautions are here to stay. So, it's time for some positive thinking. Sure, changes in sexual routine need to be made but, with imagination, these changes can lead to a most fulfilling sex life. Why not drop a line to the Terence Higgins Trust, asking for some of their excellent leaflets on this subject. But if, despite all, you continue to find safer sex boring... remember that no-one is forcing you to have sex in the first place. There are other ways of passing the time.

★

This girl that I met at a party made a big play for me and invited me back to her place. I've never had problems with women before but this time I was shattered. Try as I might, I couldn't get an erection. I'm now scared to sleep with anyone else in case the same thing happens again. Help!

Some men seem to think that their penis ought to rise to the occasion, come rain or shine. But that's the stuff of erotic literature where men are ever ready, willing and able. In real life remember that, like the rest of you, your penis is merely human and will, therefore, act accordingly. In the situation that you describe your body was telling you something. Think about it. Just because this girl made a play for you doesn't mean that you have to become her playmate. In future, would it not be wiser to get to know someone first and enter into a sexual relationship because both you and your partner choose to do so?

★

I am living alone but have a very active sex life. In fact, things are becoming silly. I am seeing four ladies at the same time. Two are older and very experienced. The other two are both young, attractive and with amazing sex drives. All sounds rosy and I enjoy the set-up but there's a big problem now. I have fallen in love with one of them. Am I weird?

Perhaps you are weird! But weird because you have fallen in love? I hardly think so. I would suggest that you are merely maturing and have come to realise that playing musical beds can be a fourth rate experience.

Congratulations!

★

Help. Please can you advise? My girlfriend doesn't seem to reach an orgasm when making love. She only does so with direct clitoral stimulation. What should I do?

Lots of people have an image of love-making which concludes with sexual intercourse and a simultaneous, rapturous explosion – the big 0. But, in truth, women vary in how easily they can reach orgasm and how these orgasms are achieved. Modern experience has shown us that most women do need direct clitoral stimulation in order to climax. 'Tis only about 30% of women who are able to climax during intercourse without any clitoral 'assistance'.

Don't get too 'orgasm fixated'. As far as I can tell you are doing just fine. Taking it in turns to climax can be just as exciting, if not more so, than mutual orgasm.

★

Could you please tell me if there is such a thing as the 'G-Spot'? My wife has read about it but says she doesn't know where it is. Can you help?

The 'G-Spot' named after Ernest Grafenberg, the gynaecologist, is said to be a wonderfully sensitive area on the anterior wall of the vagina. If the 'G-Spot' is located and stimulated in the right way, 'tis said that the lucky lady could well experience a Grafenberg orgasm.

But, does the 'G-Spot' really exist? Well, some researchers are absolutely convinced that every woman has one. Others disagree and maintain that the whole of the anterior wall inside the vagina is a highly sensitive area.

I guess that you and your wife will have to do some research for yourselves and draw your own conclusions. Have an interesting time.

2
Food, Fetishes and Fantasy

A letter in this chapter from a girl dissatisfied with her once a month liaison with a recently separated man, reminds me of another recently separated man who crossed my path some years ago. His story was much the same. 'I need my space' ... 'I can't cope with commitment at the moment' ... 'I think I am a loner at heart' etc ... etc...

And why do I reflect upon this long lost friend, I hear you ask? Only because my most vivid memory of him relates to his fascinating words on the subject matter of this chapter. 'I've far more fears than fantasies,' he told me, 'about meeting a woman with whom I could have a meaningful relationship. My only fantasy now would run along the lines of *Last Tango in Paris* but without the butter. Polyunsaturated sex with no strings attached.' One person's thoughts for you. More on the way!.

★

Recently during my sleep, I am experiencing strange dreams which include me fantasising about making love with famous film stars. Is this normal?

Depends who the film stars are, doesn't it? If you started fantasising about Lassie, for example, I'd start to worry! Only joking, my friend. You sound like a perfectly healthy, well-adjusted human being. Sweet dreams!

★

I am a very shy and retiring young lady of good breeding who is sexually attracted to the dustmen in my neighbourhood and find rubbish, as a whole, a great turn on. However, I do not think this is a very healthy craving and need something to wean me off the habit. What do you suggest?

Whilst there is nothing wrong with dustmen, to be totally obsessed by them and find rubbish a great turn on is, to put it mildly, a trifle unusual. Perhaps you are attracted to dustmen as a rebellion against your good breeding. Perhaps you see sex itself as something dirty, hence your interest/ambivalence in dirt. Perhaps, you are taking the mickey. But, if your letter is genuine, let me refer you to the wise words of my father who was only saying the other day that 'zeal without prudence is frenzy'. How about some therapy? It might lead to a new you – less frenzied and more prudently zealous. That's my suggestion.

★

My husband is terribly keen on bananas and wants me to use banana flavoured boob drops. Do you think he's odd?

Boob drops come in little bottles and can be purchased at any sex shop. A drop on each nipple and your man will be over the moon – well, that's if you believe the sales talk! I certainly don't think your husband is odd 'cos he wants to try out something new. He obviously just wants you to drive him bananas!

★

My boyfriend likes me to tickle his fancy with a feather-duster. I enjoy doing this but do you think it's a strange thing to do?

Does it matter what I think? He likes it and you enjoy doing it. You are two birds of a feather. No problem! Just make sure, though, that you stick with the soft variety. I don't suppose that feather dusters are made out of the stiff plumage of the heron, for example, but, if they were, your boyfriend might find a dusting of this type, a trifle uncomfortable!

★

Please help me because I don't know what to do about my problem. I've always had a big interest in ladies' underwear but recently it's got so bad that I've started stealing knickers from my neighbour's washing line. I've never had sex with a woman but I do masturbate frequently and my neighbour's knickers make me feel very randy. In other respects I am a normal person with a good job, home of my own etc.

It's not uncommon for a person, particularly a member of the male species, to develop a fetish about a specific item of clothing. Could it be that you have worries about your sexual performance and find that your 'knickers fetish' provides you with the opportunity to retreat from the world of adult sexuality? Fetishism often finds its roots in childhood and for your benefit, not to mention that of your neighbours (knickers are not cheap these days!), I would recommend that you seek professional help. Once you begin to unravel and understand past experiences, you may well start to overcome your present difficulties.

★

My girlfriend has taken a liking to walking through mud in her bare feet and she says it turns her on. I tried it and felt the same way as her. Is this normal?

I have spent several hours looking through my textbooks on human sexuality but can find nothing relating to the effects of walking through mud on sexual arousal. So, to answer your question .... is this normal? .... who knows and, frankly, who cares? You and your girlfriend are obviously having fun. As long as you continue to enjoy yourselves and don't tread mud all over the carpet, I can't honestly see that you have a problem.

★

I got this boyfriend. Well, I call him my boyfriend but I only see him about once a month. He keeps telling me he needs his space and always has an excuse for not seeing me. When he does show up the sex is not so great because he often can't perform. My friend told me the other day that she thinks this man is my fantasy because there's not a lot going on. Could you comment please? I'm not sure how to improve the situation. By the way, he was married for a long time and split up from his wife six months ago.

I'm not so sure that you are in a position to improve the situation with this man. From where I'm typing, sounds like he's stuck in the 'not too trigger-happy Lone Ranger Syndrome' – commonly experienced by chaps emerging from a long and disappointing previous liaison. He's still mourning the loss of his marriage, is not ready to commit himself again but likes a bit of company as and when the mood takes him. Your friend could well be right in telling you that this man is a fantasy for you. You certainly don't have a real, substantial relationship on your hands now, do you? Only you can decide whether you want to continue on this tantalising trip, bearing in mind that you could be going nowhere slowly.

★

I always thought that bagels were Jewish bread rolls until my wife told me that she wanted to make love in the bagel position! What is she going on about?

The bagel is a Jewish bread roll, shaped like a polo with a hole in the middle. Delicious eaten hot with smoked salmon. If you fancy making your own, look up the recipe in Florence Greenberg's cookery book. The bègles position is something else, however, and not a subject that Mrs. Greenberg ever wrote about! If you want the recipe, you'll have to seek it out in *The SHE Complete Guide to Sex & Loving* by Doc Delvin.

★

My boyfriend always spends a lot of time tickling my feet. I really enjoy it but am wondering whether he's kinky. What do you think?

Listen, in eighteenth century Russia, the Tsarina put enormous effort into employing her official foot-ticklers. She never wrote to a Sex Therapist asking if they were kinky or not! I can only say that, if your boyfriend likes to tickle and you enjoy being tickled, then you aint gotta problem. If, however, it reaches the stage that your boyfriend only pays attention to your feet and begins to neglect your other bits and pieces, write to me again. An interest in one part of the body becomes far more problematic if you, as an individual, become redundant.

★

I have been married for 22 years and have always been a loyal husband. Recently, I was made redundant and my next door neighbour, a lovely girl in her 20s, has taken to inviting me in for coffee. Yesterday she told me that she finds older men very sexy and that I really turn her on. I made a quick exit but it wasn't easy and I can't stop fantasising about her. How am I going to resist her?

Mind over matter, my friend. If you love your wife and want your marriage to continue, it wouldn't be a clever move to have a little number with the next-door neighbour, lovely though she might be. Make sure that your fantasies stay where they belong and get back to the realities of every day life. Look for a job if you want one, mow the lawn and do whatever you can to stay out of your neighbour's way. And, if it's true that older men are very sexy ... well, your wife has been around for a long time ... ensure that she reaps the benefits!

★

My mother's got this friend who keeps coming round and eating my meals before I get home from work. Yesterday she finished off my gravy. Today she ate all my potatoes and stuffing and I had to make do with roast beef, yorkshire pudding and peas. I am only skinny and will look anorexic if she doesn't stop. Can you help?

A hungry man is an angry man, for sure, but calm down for one minute and let's see what we can come up with. This woman friend of your mothers could have all manner of deep-rooted problems. What they are, I do not know. But what I do know is that she sounds hungry with a capital H. Be big-hearted and allow a little gravy etc. to flow in her direction. It's probably only a temporary phase anyway and highly unlikely that your mother will allow you to fade away in the midst of it.

★

How can I persuade my wife to wear stockings more often instead of tights?

If it's really important to you, you'll have to instigate a stocking shopping spree. Perhaps you ought to wait for a special occasion like a birthday or wedding anniversary – then suggest to your wife that you go to the most expensive shop in town to acquire the said items. Present them to her as if they were a beautiful bouquet or diamond ring. Next step – back to the ranch where you can compliment her on her terrific tibias, stockinged of course, before initiating a little light love-making. And Bob's your ankle – a wife seduced by stocking-fashion. Then again, you could have a wife who thinks you've gone off your rocker but that's the chance you've got to take.

★

My husband likes me to dress in nurses uniform which I find distressing and perform sexual acts which I think are perverted. Please advise me as I don't think that I can take much more.

If you find your husband's sexual preferences abhorrent then say so and don't take part in them. Sex is all about sharing and caring and no-one should be forced to participate in activities which they consider to be perverted.

Is your marriage successful in other respects? If so, you ought to be able to overcome this problem by talking together and discovering mutually pleasing aspects of sexuality. You could also think about contacting RELATE, formerly the Marriage Guidance Council, for counselling help.

★

After I have sex with my wife, I get the urge to eat pork pies. Can you explain why this happens?

Given my basic faith in human nature, I'm assuming that your letter is genuine. Now, had you wanted me to explain why you could only have sex after eating pork pies, the answer would be simple. You would be suffering from the very rare condition known as 'the pork pie fetish!' But sex before pies? I can only conclude that sex makes you hungry and you are particularly partial to pork. I sincerely hope that you are not expecting your wife to slave over the stove all day long and bake the objects in question, that it's not against your religion to eat them and that you're not making a pig of yourself. No further comment.

★

I am a student of agriculture. Due to my leanings towards livestock, I constantly find myself drifting away from my studies and fantasising about sheep. Please help me as these thoughts may turn into actual passionate actions.

Stop subscribing to the *Stockbreeders' Gazette* and buy *Playboy* immediately!

★

I read a lot of Mills and Boon novels and keep falling in love with the tall, dark, arrogant heroes. My boyfriend now seems very ordinary by comparison and I am getting bored with him. Am I being silly?

Frankly, yes. By all means continue to read romantic fiction if you enjoy it, but there seems little point in comparing your boyfriend to a tall, dark, arrogant non-existent hero. Your boyfriend may well be ordinary but at least he's alive and kicking which means that, if you are dissatisfied with the relationship, you can sit down and talk with him. Why don't you do just that and see where it leads?

★

My boyfriend and I like to play sex games with food. I am a vegetarian while he is a meat-eater and the thought of sausages makes me ill. I prefer a stuffed marrow any day. How can we compromise? Meat and two veg?

For someone with a great sense of humour, your lack of imagination surprises me. Have you never given any thought to stuffed vegetarian sausages, available at all health food shops?!

★

I am a 19 year old and want to know why, when I talk to the male species, they talk back to my boobs. I feel as though my face is on my chest. Help, because it is so embarrassing.

Not all men see women as being of anatomical interest only. But it sounds to me like you are coming into contact with that type of male or, alternatively, the shy and retiring sort who can't tolerate direct eye contact.

In any event, it's up to you to teach these chaps that your face is not on your chest. Think positive and assume that men are potentially capable of raising an eye or two. Startle them with your confidence, fascinating conversation or whatever. Or just go for the direct approach. Something like 'Now, look here mate. It's about time we saw eye to eye'.

★

I am a diagnosed nymphomaniac and fantasise non-stop about every aspect of sex. My doctor says there is nothing he can do to help me. Please could you recommend someone I could see?

When a woman's sexual desire is so strong that sex becomes a constant obsession, the condition is called nymphomania, named after the Greek goddess of love. Well, that's what they say in the text books anyway! Personally, I am not convinced that this condition exists. If it does, it is so rare that you, a diagnosed nymphomaniac, would be a medical curiosity. With all due respect, my friend, I think you are having me on!

★

I have a big problem. I manage a shop and I fantasise about dressing up in the girls' uniforms. Sometimes I even try them on before they come into work and it really turns me on. I don't think I am gay but I do feel good in women's clothes. Is this just a phase? Please tell me as it's driving me mad.

Transvestism or cross-dressing, a desire to dress up in the clothes of the opposite sex, is a phenomenon which has occurred throughout history. Some people dress up in order to get sexually aroused, but many do so simply because they find it relaxing. You may be going through a phase, but it's not necessarily the case. Certain men consistently indulge in cross-dressing; others find it a comforting activity during times of stress. Contact the Beaumont Society which offers a counselling service for transvestites and the opportunity to cross-dress in company.

★

Can you tell me anything about Spanish Flea?

Spanish Flea, as I recall, was a perfectly harmless little melody recorded by Herb Alpert and the Tijuana Brass. But I think that you might be confusing your fleas with your flies! Spanish Fly is the name given to the drug cantharides. It's a so-called aphrodisiac which is extremely dangerous and could kill you.

*Some months ago, I wrote to you about a sexual problem that I was having
with my wife. I took your advice, went to see a Sex Therapist and now I have
another problem. I have fallen wildly in love with my Sex Therapist. I have
not, of course, discussed this with my wife. My sex life is now fantastic but
only because I fantasise that I'm in bed with my therapist. If my wife knew,
she'd go mad. What do you think I ought to do? Is it all very abnormal?*

No. It's not abnormal at all. It is a well-known psychological
phenomenon that some people fall in love with their therapists and
therapists are fully aware that this occurs. They are also aware that
sometimes clients use them as 'punch-bags' – venting their anger
upon them in place of the people in their lives who, in their
understanding, have caused their problems.

This is what therapy is all about – the intimacy and intensity of
the relationship are part of the therapeutic process. If your feelings of
love for your therapist don't fade, it might be wise to discuss them with
her. Meanwhile, fantasising about your therapist won't do any harm,
providing that you continue to keep your dreams to yourself.

3

Sexual Problems from Women

It was at a lecture on 'Idealism versus Dialectical Materialism' that a fellow told me he'd lost his manhood during a Tory cut and was having to make-do with a nuclear-powered prosthetic. Sounded a little far-fetched to me so I didn't display too much sympathy but his words did make me ponder.

Letters from my male readers frequently dwell upon what's below their belts. Sexual problems from women, when you study them, are mainly about their men.

Why can't a man be more like a woman? That's what I want to know ...

★

My husband and I get on very well and sexually things are good but he gets upset if I don't have an orgasm when he does during intercourse. He tries his best but it doesn't always work out! Any advice?

Penetration is not the name of the game! Far too often sex is spoiled by a chap's heroic efforts to ensure that his partner comes when he does. But the majority of women have orgasms when the clitoris is stimulated and not on penile penetration alone. Tell your husband not to work too hard. If it happens, it happens. Many people prefer to take turns when it comes to coming. In this way, they can focus on their individual pleasure. And, remember, there's more to life than the Big O. If, sometimes, you don't have one, then who gives an orgasm!

★

My husband only ever touches me when we make love. He would never ever consider giving me a hug, just for the sake of it. How can I change him?

I don't have much faith in the old proverb that 'a good wife makes a good husband' (it would take at least another book to explain why!) but I do believe that we can teach our men a thing or two. In this instance, it wouldn't be a bad idea to give your husband a course of lessons in the art of sensuality. Regrettably, too many men in our culture think that physical contact is acceptable only between the sheets or on the rugby field – it's too bad, for them and us.

Take the initiative and hug him from time to time. Offer a massage and get him to return the favour. If you can slowly introduce some non-sexual touching (non-demand snuggling, as the American Sexperts call it!) into your lives, you may find that your husband begins to indulge in tactile pleasures. Okay? I'll leave this matter in your capable hands!

★

A while back, my husband became the goalkeeper of the local football team. This seems to be taking up all his energy and our sex life has gone down the drain. All I get these days is a very quick quickie ! What am I going to do?

The occasional quickie can be quite thrilling but, if your husband is constantly quick on the draw, I can understand that it would become somewhat tedious. Tea for two and a chat, don't you think? Tell him that there's a lot more to a goalie's job than kicking the ball into the other half.... and see what he says. If he doesn't hearken to reason, perhaps you could arrange for him to be temporarily transferred to Glasgow Rangers. But I hope it won't come to that!

★

I often take a dominant role in our love making. My husband seems happy enough for me to do this but I'm wondering whether there is something wrong with me. I enjoy our sex life very much but sometimes I think I ought to be more passive and let him do more of the work.

Well, I don't think that there is anything wrong with you.

Look, you say that you and your husband are both happy with your sex life... so what's the problem? Certainly, the old, stereotyped images taught us that men took total responsibility for the seduction and whatever else that followed, whilst the woman passively reclined and did little but look appealing. But that's the stuff of Hollywood movies. In real life, if love making is shared and not something that one person does to another, it's bound to be more pleasurable for both concerned.

★

I have been married for four years but my husband and I still haven't had proper sex. I went to the doctor who examined me and said I had vaginismus. He was going to discuss this with a colleague and get in touch with me but he didn't do this. I am desperate. Can you advise?

Vaginismus is a condition which is responsible for many non-consummated marriages. What happens is that the ring of muscles surrounding the vaginal entrance go into spasm and shut tight, making it impossible for the penis to enter. Sometimes this can be traced back to a traumatic sexual experience - other times there is no such obvious cause. But what's important is that it is a learned condition which can be unlearned and responds well to treatment. Go back to your GP and ask to be referred to a Sex Therapist. If he cannot make a suitable referral, contact the Association of Sexual and Marital Therapists for details of therapists in your area.

★

My husband and I have been married for a long time. We always make love in the missionary position but we now feel like experimenting. Any suggestions?

Well, firstly, let me say that there's nothing wrong with the missionary position which is a very popular one. As Dr Ruth says: 'If you think of a sexual repertoire as a kind of cuisine, this is the meat and potatoes of it!' But there's a lot to be said for a varied menu and vegetables, of course, are extremely nourishing. Try and find other positions which you both find comfortable. If you feel that a little night reading on this matter would not go amiss, take an hour or two off and browse through your local book shop for some literature on this fascinating subject. Have fun.

★

I have been seeing my boyfriend for 9 months and I have grown very fond of him. But, just the other night, while we were lovemaking, he asked me to turn over on my stomach, so I did and he had anal sex with me. Afterwards I was very distressed. If he wants to do it again, should I go along with it?

No. Your boyfriend is ignoring the sexual commandment... 'Thou shalt only practise what is pleasurable and accepted by you and your partner.' Thrusting anal sex upon you when it's not your bag, as we used to say in the olden days, is definitely not on. Make your feelings known to him and, if he's as fond of you as you are of him, he ought to respect your views on the subject.

★

I've been married for four years. I've never ever had an orgasm and I've got into the habit of pretending that I climax to please my husband. But I am beginning to feel very frustrated. What should I do? It's not going to be easy to tell my husband the truth after all this time.

If you continue to let your husband think you are having orgasms, there's not much chance that you will improve the situation. It might not be easy to bring up this subject, but it is in your interest to do so and ultimately, will be in your husband's interest too. Alternatively, if you stop pretending that you are having orgasms, it's possible that your husband will raise the issue in due course. As you've never reached a climax, it would be helpful if you could explore your own body and learn how to masturbate yourself to orgasm. You should then be able to guide your husband in the techniques that satisfy you.

★

I have had sexual intercourse with my boyfriend three times and, although I like what goes on before, I don't seem to enjoy penetration. Is there something wrong with me?

No. It is quite common for women to enjoy the pre-coital aspects of lovemaking such as touching, kissing and clitoral stimulation, yet feel rather disappointed with the first few penetrations. Sexual intercourse does tend to improve with practice and it may take a while before you feel sufficiently confident and relaxed to enjoy it. Never have sexual intercourse unless you truly want to do so and try not to feel embarrassed about telling your partner what turns you on. If you can share your anxieties as well as your positive feelings with your partner, I am sure that your relationship will flourish.

★

I love my husband very much but I'm afraid to say that he's not very sexy. Whereas I'd love to have sex every night, his interest in sex is now virtually non-existent and it's getting to the stage that we only make love on our anniversary! What should I do? I can't stand this for much longer.

It would have been helpful had you told me your ages, how long you've been together and when your husband's interest in sex started to wane. Has he ever had a more active interest in sex? Have you been sexually dissatisfied from the start of your relationship? Have you talked together about the state of your sex life? Look, this isn't going to be an easy problem to resolve but I do feel that you might be helped by seeing a good Sex Therapist to discuss some of these issues. I doubt that your husband will ever want to have sex as often as you do, but if you are both committed to your marriage, you may reach a compromise.

★

I am a 21 year old girl with a problem. Ever since I got married four months ago, I've gone right off sex. Yet, before my marriage, I had an active sex life and no problems. Can you help?

One of the most commonly believed myths which seems to give rise to sexual problems for many couples is that nice, respectable married women shouldn't have sexual feelings. Does this ring any bells for you? Was sex more enjoyable prior to your marriage because you saw yourself as 'less respectable' and, therefore, allowed yourself to be sexual? Whatever the case, I'd suggest that you arrange to see a Sex Therapist now and talk through your problems rather than let them continue and become more difficult to sort out. It's most encouraging that you enjoyed sex before your marriage and I see no reason why, with some counselling, you should not resume a satisfying sex life.

★

I am a 26 year old with a small problem. I look after my next door neighbour and, although he is 75, still find myself in his bed at least twice a week. I have a steady boyfriend who I love but who just doesn't satisfy me in the way this other man does. I desperately need advice on what to do. Should I tell my boyfriend he has a bit of competition or shall I just let it go on?

Listen, my friend, no woman 'finds' herself in bed with the man next door. You have chosen to have sex with him because, according to you, your boyfriend is not satisfying you. Whether or not you tell your boyfriend how well you look after your neighbour is up to you but you must sit down and talk with him. Love aside, discover if you and he can form a working relationship. You may decide you can. You may decide you can't. You might like a spell on your own. Perhaps you will continue to love thy neighbour. Work out what is right for you and don't play musical beds – you risk spreading a sexually transmitted disease.

★

Do you think there are any men who can cope with equality? All of the ones I meet seem to want to dominate me but I'm an independent woman and don't want that kind of a relationship. Does the 'new man' really exist? I can't seem to find one with whom to have a complete emotional and sexual relationship.

Perhaps the 'new man' is a fictional creature. Can't say I've seen many around North London, where I live. But let's not give up all hope; a few 'newer men' must be emerging from the woodwork. There's no general rule without exception but it does seem as if our man of today quite likes the idea of equality, yet finds it difficult to live with. But take a look at his history. Have we not always been a chap's chattel, bought and sold by him ... even, in some South Sea islands, specially fattened and eaten by him? It's all to do with the big problem of power and the little problem of what lies in his jeans. Keep truckin', my friend. Tomorrow is another day.

★

I've got a new man in my life who is screwing me up. He seems to enjoy the chase and, for a few weeks, he was very attentive, bouquets of flowers, the whole business. But now that I've had sex with him, he's cooled off in a big way, pays me little attention and keeps telling me how much he fancies other women. I'm getting bad vibes about everything and am planning to opt out. The thing is that I feel such an idiot because I've experienced this before and don't seem to have learnt from previous errors. What's more, I am 37 years old – no baby. Can you help, Sandra? I'm so fed up.

'At the age of 37 she realised she'd never ride through Paris in a sport's car with the warm wind in her hair', sang Marianne Faithful in *The Ballad of Lucy Jordan*. But as Marianne knows only too well, life/learning doesn't stop at the age of 37. We are all growing up all of the time so don't be so hard on yourself. Your man sounds like he's suffering from the 'putting out the bait but not wanting the fish when you catch it syndrome'. He probably relished a taste of the flesh but his little stomach couldn't cope with a slap-up meal. Be smart and let this guy wander further down the river bank. You deserve something bigger and better than small fly!

★

My problem isn't very great but it is very embarrassing. I have been living with my fiancé for six months and he has developed very great sexual urges. He demands sex in the car, all night and has even made me take days off work so he can have sex with me. He also likes going into sex shops and saying out loud what I would like. I love him very much but, because of this, I am getting bored. Help.

I suppose lots of women would envy you. Your fiancé is clearly besotted by you and is expressing his love in a very physical way (though telling all the sex shop customers what you like is, in my view, definitely over the top, so insist that he shuts up!).However, if all this sex is boring you, not to mention affecting your safety, (or, does he, at least park the car before wanting sex in it?!) you should gently suggest other areas of your relationship might benefit from more attention and development. How about a trip to a football match/art gallery/cinema as an alternative to another roll in the hay? Sex is only one area of life. You need to explore other parts together too.

★

I've met this really great bloke and we've been together for three months now. Everything is terrific except for one thing. Whenever we go to bed, he always compares me with his ex-wife and talks about her orgasms and how they differ from mine. I don't want to know all this but am not sure what to do. Can you help?

Looking on the positive side, I guess it's possible that your boyfriend is not used to relating to women, apart from his ex-wife, and is unaware that such comparisons are totally tactless. On the other hand, if he continues to dwell upon the sexual performance of his ex-wife, maybe he hasn't yet got her out of his system and wants you to deal with all his leftover feelings. Either way, you end up the loser, wondering whether he's in bed with you or her. I can only suggest that you tell him how upsetting it is and see what he says. If he wants your liaison to continue, he'll presumably attempt to break the pattern.

★

My sex life is fine, I think, but my boyfriend has started to get very anxious if I don't have an orgasm at the same time as he does. This doesn't bother me, but he thinks that he's doing something wrong. Is he? Also, very occasionally, I don't even have an orgasm!

I doubt it. It sounds like he's creating problems where they don't exist, so perhaps you should put him straight. Statistics from our friends, the American sexperts, clearly display that only about 30% of women climax during penetration alone. Most women have orgasms when the clitoris is stimulated. So tell your boyfriend to stop worrying. If a mutual orgasm happens, it happens. If it doesn't, then taking turns to climax can be as enjoyable, if not more so, than climaxing together. And please don't think I'm knocking orgasms, but, if you don't have one today, does it matter? Who knows what tomorrow will bring?

★

Whenever my husband and I make love, he always starts by touching my toes and then works upwards. My best friend told me that her husband always starts at the top and goes down. Is there a right way of doing things?

Of course not. I personally believe that variety gives a wife her spice but you and your partner should do whatever it is that turns you both on. There's nothing wrong with exchanging sexual ideas over a cup of coffee. By all means, keep chatting to your best friend but don't attempt to model your sexual relationship upon hers.

★

I am 25 years old and have had a lot of experience with various men. My problem is that I am unable to reach orgasm. Please advise.

If you gain more understanding of your own sexuality and learn how to give yourself an orgasm, it's likely that you will then be able to teach your partner how to satisfy you. A good book to read on this subject is *The Body Electric* by Anne Hooper. But I also think it's important to reflect upon the type of sexual encounters in which you've involved yourself in the past. You say that you've had considerable experience with various men. Perhaps the time has come to think about quality rather than quantity? A good sexual relationship often takes time to develop and, if you were to have a special relationship with one person, you might well feel sufficiently relaxed to unwind and allow yourself to reach a climax.

★

I am generally a shy, introverted type of woman but, recently, my boyfriend who is a 43 year old divorcee has suggested that we both try partner swapping. Also he wants me to talk in detail of my sexual experiences whilst we share our bed together. As you can imagine, I am most distressed about the whole affair and I don't know who or where to turn to. So please try and help me if you possible can.

Your boyfriend, in trying to impose his ideas upon you, is not playing cricket, I'm afraid. If you have no wish to discuss past sexual experiences when you are in bed with him ... and I must say I think this is perfectly understandable ... then don't do it. As for swapping partners, it's a most unfashionable business and the risks involved, particularly those of contracting a sexually transmitted disease, are considerable. All I can suggest is that you make your preferences perfectly clear to your boyfriend. If he makes it perfectly clear that he's not prepared to respect your wishes, perhaps you ought to ask yourself what you are doing in this relationship.

★

I've been seeing this guy regularly for four months. Having a great time with him but no physical contact. At first, I thought he was AIDSphobic but now I think he's scared to touch me. He sees me as this very strong woman, in control of everything. This isn't the case. I'm just a single parent of two, struggling hard to make ends meet on salary of one. I'm not strong. I'm doing what I have to do. Why's he so threatened by me?

I don't know. Perhaps he is threatened by you. Perhaps he isn't. Maybe he just doesn't want a deep involvement at the moment. Maybe he does but likes to move slowly but surely. Maybe he is AIDSphobic. Maybe he's one of a million different things. But whatever he is, you are obviously finding the virtues of patience particularly painful and don't seem happy about waiting for him to proffer the first HIV-free handshake/fond fondle and so on and so forth.

Could you not have a word in his ear and delicately raise this delicate subject? Reassure him that, if he pricks you, you'll bleed. Such a discussion could lead to lust rearing its beautiful head. Or it could make you realise that this man is not for you ... not, that is, in a sexual sense. One way or t'other, I hope it works out. Do keep in touch.

★

After 12 years of marriage, my husband and I are still virgins. We are both 37. My husband had a very strict upbringing and seems to be disgusted with the idea of love-making. I keep suggesting that we get help, but he won't agree. I have recently met another man and am thinking about having sex with him. Do you think that this would be very wrong?

Am I right in assuming that, as you've stayed with your husband for twelve years, certain aspects of your partnership are successful? If this is the case and you do care about your husband, then it might be worth giving him an ultimatum ... one final chance to consult Relate (formerly the Marriage Guidance Council) or a Sex Therapist. If your husband still refuses to seek professional help, then only you can work out how important it is for you to enter into a sexual relationship. You may well come to the conclusion that you have no alternative but to do so outside of your marriage.

★

My boyfriend has just returned from New York and he has brought me back some Geisha balls as a gift. What are they? I can't work out what to do with them.

Well, I'm not surprised! Geisha or Duo balls, as they are also called, consist of two balls joined together by a thread. Believe it or not, whoever invented them did so with the intention that women insert them into their vaginas when in need of sexual stimulation. If you are not very keen on keeping the balls rolling in this fashion, might I suggest that you attempt to convert them into earrings?!

4

Office Relations

The age of automation is upon us. But, between the hardware and the software crammed into most offices these days, one can still spot the common or garden, walking, talking humanoid. And, wherever you have common or garden, walking, talking humanoids, you have love, hate and all manner of emotions in-between.

Not surprising, is it, when the average working person spends as many waking hours inside as outside the office?

So, it's 'Office Relations' – often as complicated and intense as family dynamics.

Read all about it!

★

A colleague of mine at work, who's married with seven children under the age of nine, has asked me out for a drink. He says it's purely platonic with no strings attached. He wants to give me a helping hand regarding a work project I'm involved in. I'm unattached and find him very attractive. Help!

Okay. Let's look at this logically. He's married with seven children. You are unattached, possibly looking for a relationship and find him attractive. He's invited you out for a purely platonic drink with no strings. My advice is going to be predictable but what can you expect? You've got to agree that this situation is a recipe for disaster. Find another drinking partner quickly and tell this bloke to save his helping hands for changing the nappies.

★

I have just left school and started a new job. There is this older woman in the office who seems keen on me and I don't know what to do. She is married but wants me to go away with her for a weekend. She is very pretty and has, apparently, slept with lots of men in the office. I am a virgin. Please help me.

From the tone of your letter, I would guess that this woman scares you a little but I would advise caution for another reason altogether; if she has slept with most of the men in the office, the chances of her having and passing on a sexually transmitted disease are pretty high. Steer well clear of her. You'd only be another scalp on her belt anyway, and where's the fun in that? Tell her politely that you're not interested and stick with your virginity for the time being. I'm sure that someone more appropriate will show up in due course.

★

I am a female accountant in an all male office. The problem is that my boss is always asking me to make the coffee and pick up his suits from the dry cleaners. I like my job but not this aspect of it. How can I put a stop to this without offending him?

By being more assertive. Confront your boss directly in a polite but firm manner, and tell him, in your own words, that you enjoy your work but have neither the time nor inclination to be his hand-maiden. With luck, your boss will appreciate your honesty and see the error of his ways.

★

The secretary in our workplace is a compulsive exhibitionist who enjoys teasing all the males in the office by wearing the skimpiest of clothes. The problem has worsened due to the recent warm weather, with the effect that I feel I might succumb to my sexual desires and openly molest her while at work. What should I do as she is a total stranger to me?

Don't be so silly. Nobody succumbs to sexual desires against his will. This is the excuse that all rapists make, but it won't wash. If you like this woman, ask her out and take things from there. You may well find that she is looking for a good, steady relationship. If you don't like her, then ignore her. Or, just continue to enjoy her teasing but don't blame her appearance for your sexual desires.

★

I work in a travel agents and last week I met this boy who I really liked. He was so nice at first and bought me a red rose after I had booked his holiday for him. The next day he came back into the office and asked me out. I agreed. We went out last night in a foursome and he changed completely. First, he turned up nearly an hour late. Then, when we went out, he chatted up nearly every girl in sight. Then he wanted me to start a fight with another girl. I also found out that, before he goes on holiday, he is in a competition to get as many girls as he can. What should I do?

I once had a boyfriend who called for me on a first date, walked straight into the kitchen and did all the washing up. I thought he was terrific until the second date when it became apparent that his domestic expertise was merely a ploy. He was looking for a month's free accommodation whilst the builders were fixing his dry rot. Like the washing up, your red rose was not a declaration of true love but a means to an end. This boy is only interested in impressing his friends and boosting his silly ego. We women deserve better! Forget this chap and look around for someone who is worthy of you.

★

Please help me. I am leaving my job on Friday as I cannot stand being near my boss and not being able to tell him how I feel. What do you suggest I do? We are all going out for a farewell drink on Friday night. Please help as I don't know what to do.

Are you leaving your job because you've fallen for your boss and he's not available? If so, there seems little point in declaring your feelings for him at the farewell party. Best to make a clean break, lick your wounds and start afresh.

If, however, he is footloose and fancy free, why not make a gentle pass at him and see what happens? You've got nothing to lose, my friend, and, if things don't go according to plan, at least you won't have to face him at work on Monday morning. Good luck and do keep me posted!

★

We have a work friend who has a problem. She comes into the office in the morning with body odour. Another woman we work with says it's stale sex, as she is always late and boasts about her sex life with her husband. How can we tell her about this without embarrassing her or ourselves?

It is virtually impossible to tell someone that they have BO without hurting their feelings. Personal criticism is very hard to take calmly and maturely, although some people can handle it.

I'd suggest that you choose the most willing, tactful and sensitive person in the office to talk with her. This person will have to raise the subject of body odour and if she/he is particularly brave, could also refer to the boring nature of the sexual boasts – if you find them boring, that is. Alternatively, there's the indirect approach. Sweet smelling soap as a birthday present? But, in my humble opinion, face to face discussion, painful though it might prove to be, will produce better results.

★

I am 18 and work in an office with a team of people all approximately the same age as me. We are all good friends and often socialise with each other after work. About a month ago one of the girls I work with indicated to me that she would like to form a relationship with me. At present I am already involved in a long term relationship. The girl I work with will not take no for an answer. What should I do?

I think you have to be quite firm with your colleague and make it absolutely clear that you are not available to have a relationship with her. If you consistently reject her, I'm sure she will eventually take the hint and understand that she has to take no for an answer. Admittedly, as you are working with each other, this won't be an easy situation to handle but I doubt that it will last for very much longer. Once your colleague realises that you are not willing to play ball, it's likely she'll move her attentions elsewhere and you'll discover you were just a passing fancy!

★

I have this awful problem with the girls I work with. I can't keep my hands off them. I know this makes me sound like a dirty old man but I can't help it. When they reject my advances, I get really upset and I take it out on my steady girlfriend at home. Please help as I'm really getting desperate.

Have you tried to understand why you can't keep your hands off the girls at work? Is it because your self-esteem is so low that it has to be bolstered by every woman you come into contact with? Are you linking individual worth with sexual attractiveness? If so, it's no wonder you take out each rejection on your girlfriend. Your self-confidence is non-existent and you probably despise her for being with you in the first place. To need such constant and obvious reassurance is desperate and very sad indeed. May I take this opportunity of reminding you that you are working in an office, not a harem. Sexual relationships are not the only relationships and you are in danger of becoming a bore. If you cannot understand and overcome your compulsion, seek professional help.

★

I am having an affair with a man I work with and have my husband's consent. The affair is just lustful … no emotions involved. My husband keeps telling me he wants to hear about sexual acts that happen between my lover and I but I've always kept quiet. Sandra, please tell me what to do.

While it may sound sophisticated that you have your husband's consent to pursue a little lust on the side, it doesn't sound kosher to me and could lead to dreary marital problems. Only you can decide if you want to continue in this affair and titillate your husband, or whether you'd prefer to take a deeper look at your marriage, working out why you need extra-marital lust and why your husband needs to hear about it. If you decide upon the latter, you may wish to incorporate the help of the professional.

★

I was recently a very straight man but, after a long period without a girlfriend, I have started a gay affair with my best mate at work. The problem is everyone knows he is gay and has had many gay partners. How would I find out if he has AIDS or any other kind of VD as I intend to carry on the affair but without catching anything?

The only way of finding out whether or not someone has the AIDS virus is for them to undergo the HIV antibody test. This test is available in all Sexually Transmitted Diseases (STD) Clinics. It's not a test for AIDS and cannot predict if a person will become ill. As for STDs in general, sometimes obvious symptoms develop; sometimes they don't. Your friend may be willing to be tested for the whole gamut of STDs at a clinic but it's his decision.

As you are planning to continue in this relationship, willy-nilly, I would strongly suggest that you take safer sex precautions.

★

I am always being chatted up by blokes who come into the office. The only thing is that I want to take them to bed … all at the same time! How can I cure my sexual drive or do I just submit to my desires?

Group sex, my friend, is no longer fashionable. So it looks like you will have to 'cure your sexual drive', doesn't it? For starters, could you not distract yourself by working at the office?!

'Call for you, Miss Merrytime... Shall I hold?'

★

I was having this affair with a man at work. I really loved him a lot. The problem is that we had a very big argument and he accepted a transfer to another office in Europe. This was three months ago. We write occasionally but we never mention either our affair or the bust-up. I'm very confused. I really want to see him again but don't know how to bring up the subject and I don't know if he wants to see me. Does this make any sense? Can you help?

This is a classic case of unfinished business. You separated in the middle of an affair and were not given the opportunity to talk through your differences. All is not lost, however. You've not lost the art of letter writing, I trust, and there's no reason why you shouldn't write to this man and simply say that you would like to see him. Europe may not be round the corner but it isn't Australia. If he wants to see you, I'm sure you could meet half-way. Obviously, you take the risk that you might not get a positive response from him. But running your life without taking the occasional risk would be rather dull, don't you think?

★

I am a married woman with two children aged 14 and 15. During the past four years, my husband and I have not had sex and I have found someone who works in the same office, with whom I have been having an affair for the past three years. I enjoy his company and his lovemaking. Last month, thinking that my children had gone swimming, my lover visited me and we made love in the lounge. To my horror, the children arrived to catch us in the act. They left immediately but have threatened to tell my husband. Until now, nothing has happened but I am a nervous wreck, awaiting the moment when my husband will explode. What should I do now?

Sooner or later the truth will come out – better sooner than later, in my opinion. Rather than await your husband's explosion and, in the process, become a nervous wreck, I would advise you to raise the subject now. If you don't, your children might do so and that would be even worse. It would appear that your marriage has been on the rocks for some considerable time and that you have found consolation in your colleague. Only by talking openly with your husband will you be able to discover whether or not your marriage is beyond repair and with whom, if anyone, your future lies.

★

I've recently started going out with a boy (two weeks ago) who I met through work. We've had a good time so far, kissed and cuddled, but he hasn't tried to have sex with me. Do you think he has sexual problems? Is there something wrong with him? I really want a good sexual relationship.

Come now ... give the man a break! Surely you can't genuinely believe that your boyfriend has sexual problems because he has not yet attempted to enter into a full sexual relationship with you. Allow it to develop at its own pace and don't force the issue. Two weeks of kissing and cuddling means that he is slowly but surely getting to know you. In these circumstances, my friend, patience is a virtue. Enjoy the beginning of your friendship and don't precipitate a hasty ending by losing your cool and jumping off at the deep end.

★

I have just discovered that my husband is having an affair with his secretary. He says that this relationship doesn't mean very much to him, yet he refuses to give her up. I don't know what to do. I work with a young man who is always eyeing me up. Do you think I ought to encourage him and get back at my husband in this way? Nothing I am doing at present seems to be helping. My husband seems to want to stay in the marriage and continue his affair as well. Please help because I'm stuck.

Your husband seems to be clear about what he wants from the marriage without having considered your feelings at all. An affair with his secretary might be very convenient for him but you need to make it plain that you don't want a marriage of convenience and are finding the situation most disturbing. Before becoming involved with someone else, do try and shake your husband out of his complacency and have an honest discussion with him. If this proves difficult, you could contact RELATE, formerly the Marriage Guidance Council.

★

I have been having an affair with a man I work with but it came to an end a few weeks ago. We are still working together but I am finding the situation impossible. Every time I see him I think I am going to burst out crying, but he seems to be handling it all very well. The silly thing is that I ended the relationship for very good reasons. What's bothering me, I suppose, is that he's showing no emotion whatsoever. I don't know whether to talk to him about it or not. I'm really confused. Please help.

I imagine you ended the relationship because he was not what you wanted. Now he's not suffering enough. Perhaps he did not have the depth of feeling you were looking for and this is highlighted in his response. Or he may simply be acting a part to cover up his hurt pride. Men are particularly good at hiding their feelings; they've had a long apprenticeship. It's hard to work with someone you've had an affair with because you can't walk away, as most of us do, to lick your wounds and find the courage to start all over again. There it is ... failure staring you in the face every morning. But I doubt that he much likes the situation either. Try smiling – talk when it seems natural to do so. In time, you'll probably feel more comfortable and may even develop a friendship.

★

I've been quite happily married for the last four years to a man that I am very fond of. But, over the last six months, I have become very restless because I am developing a strong physical attraction towards a female colleague who is a lesbian. She has made it clear that she would like to get involved with me and the thought is very appealing, even though I'm nervous because I have never had sex with another woman. Do you have any advice? I can't think about anything else.

Sex *is* appealing! For many, it's even more appealing when it appears to be somehow secretive and promises new experiences. But this appeal has quite a large price tag attached. You do not say that you love your husband, simply that you are very fond of him. Is it possible that you are not receiving or giving the right amount of affection and sex to each other, and pastures new are very alluring? Look, I'd love to be able to tell you to have your cake and eat it, but that's not the way it goes. If you want your marriage to last, think long and hard before involving yourself with this woman.

★

I have developed a friendship with a man at work. I've often asked him out for a drink but he usually turns me down and seems to prefer his own company. I'm sure he's very lonely and I feel sorry for him. Please advise.

One man's loneliness is another man's solitude. What I'm trying to say is that you may well feel sorry for your friend because you wouldn't like to be in his shoes but it's quite possible that he enjoys the time he spends alone and doesn't have your desire for company. If you feel that this isn't the case, then raise the subject with him and see what develops. But don't pressurise him into adopting a life style which holds no interest for him. We all have different needs and, if you wish your friendship to continue, you must respect those of your friend.

★

I am the only male in the office and am always being harassed by the girls. What can I do as I am unable to turn down their advances?

How advanced are their advances? Are they confined to the verbal or are women constantly pinning you to the floor with no room for manoeuvre? If this is the case, my friend, perhaps you ought to take it up with your boss or the union, if you belong to one. If this isn't the case, and I don't suppose for one moment that it is, then what are you doing writing to me in the first place? I'm a busy woman, you know. It's nearly Christmas Eve and I haven't even had the time to buy the cranberries let alone, like your colleagues, get saucy.

★

I am gay and I have a serious problem. I work with another gay in my office and I am deeply attracted to him. I can't stop myself from touching him whenever I walk past and I can't seem to take my eyes off him. I think he likes my advances but can't be sure. He is involved with another man at the moment and has been for some time now. Please could you give me some advice as to whether to confront him with my love for him or not. Please help me.

If you are constantly staring at this man and touching him up, whilst at work, I would imagine that he is well aware of the fact you are deeply attracted to him. Confronting him further with your love could be rather risky, don't you think? First of all, he has a boyfriend already and is likely to reject you. Secondly, if you are even more blatant than you already have been, and he decides to reject you, it could make for a most embarrassing working relationship. The choice is yours, however. If you feel that you cannot continue as you are, then invite him for a drink and be honest, bearing in mind the consequences might not be to your liking.

★

There is this bloke at work who is gay and we all tease and laugh at him. Little do my colleagues know that I am in love with him. I guess this means that I am also gay. How can I tell him I love him? I can't cope with the situation as it is, without him knowing how I feel. Thanks for your help.

To declare your full feelings, initially, might be somewhat over-whelming for this man. Why not invite him out – for a drink, a meal or visit to the theatre – and attempt to get to know him a little better? Or you could write and ask him if he'd care to embark upon a friendship. What you must also do is stop joining your colleagues in their unpleasant teasing of this man. He's hardly likely to want to get to know you better if you are one of a group of tormentors. Since you are unsure of your own sexual direction, making friends with your colleague may be a very pleasant way of finding out where you are heading.

★

One of my colleagues seems to spend an awful lot of time in the lavatory and always asks me if he can borrow my newspaper to take with him. I find it hard to say no but am particularly fussy about hygiene and don't like the idea at all. What should I do?

Funny you should write in with, what I call 'the time in the loo' problem. One of my colleagues is exactly the same, except he likes to borrow my fascinating tomes on sexual functioning. I solved the problem by changing my literature. When, for example, I offered him *Plumbing, Gasfitting and Sewage Disposal – A Beginner's Guide*, he disdainfully disappeared, making it perfectly apparent that I was in his bad books. Get the picture?

5

Teenage Troubles

When my youngest daughter turned into a teenager a couple of years ago, I made the huge error of ordering a Tarzangram for her birthday. In the midst of a well wicked whoobub, Tarzan arrived in a clapped-out Mini Clubman Estate.

French speaking and furtively moving, he crept into the kitchen and removed his long black leather coat to reveal himself in practically all his glory.

Alas, there was no time for monkey-punky. The birthday girl was terrified, rushed to her room and promptly wrote to Claire Rayner for some good advice.

It's not easy being a teenager.

★

My boyfriend and I split up three weeks ago and I have just heard that he has already found another girlfriend. I can't believe that he has done this so quickly and I feel really angry towards him. I feel like throwing a brick through his window. I don't suppose I'll do this but what can I do to make myself feel better?

I would think that your boyfriend has chosen a well known panacea to get over his feelings for you – a relationship on the rebound. If it's any consolation, however, what we don't resolve in one relationship, we tend to confront next time around. I can imagine that you do feel like throwing a brick through his window but it's not a very good idea, is it? Instead, take up any interesting invitations that come your way, and try to do something new and creative, preferably something you couldn't do while you were with him. That will make you feel better.

★

I have erections every day (at least three times a day). In school my penis becomes erect and I can't control it. Is there something wrong with me?

Lots of boys, once they reach the age of eleven or so, find that they start to have spontaneous erections, both during the day and the night. This is a perfectly natural and healthy occurrence although I do appreciate that it can be somewhat embarrassing at times. All I can say is that, after a while, unwanted erections do tend to stop happening. Meanwhile, please don't worry because there is absolutely nothing wrong with you.

★

My son has just turned 14. He is a very gentle boy and never seems to fit in with the crowd. He gets on very well with girls and has no problem in forming a relationship with them. The only problem is that the girls say they find him unusual in that he is more interested in their personalities than their bodies. I have found that other boys make fun of him and have had a psychiatric report which says that both he and his brain are of the feminine gender. What do I do now? His father loves him.

I find it very surprising that a psychiatrist should label a 14 year old boy in this way. We are all a mixture of the so-called masculine and feminine qualities and we also develop at different stages. In my experience, it is quite normal for a 14 year old boy not to be interested in girls' bodies. In fact, I would think it is more healthy for him to be interested in girls as people, which they are, rather than as sexual objects. This will stand him in very good stead when he forms a relationship later on. You describe your son as a gentle, sensitive person and I would guess he is intelligent. Give him the space to grow in his own individual way and stop hindering him with stereotypes of masculine and feminine behaviour.

★

I've got myself into a bit of a mess. I'm 16 and I've sort of landed myself with an unwanted 12 year old girlfriend. We've enjoyed some physical contact and perhaps I got a bit carried away. I have no emotional feelings for her at all and find it slightly embarrassing to be with a 12 year old. In short, there is no way the relationship can work and I know it is up to me to finish it. However her family and mine are very friendly so it would be very bad to hurt her. Can you help?

This is a bit of a mess and I think you need to extract yourself from it as soon as you possibly can. I do not know what kind of physical contact you have enjoyed with this girl but you must remember that she is below the age of consent. It is a criminal offence to have sexual intercourse with a female who is under the age of 16. What's more, you say that you don't have any emotional feelings for her. Talk with her and, in as kindly a way as you can, you must end the relationship. Perhaps she will be hurt but I guess that she'll recover. I certainly hope that she will and I also hope that you'll start socialising with girls of your own age.

★

My best friend Annie had an affair with someone called Dave, for six months. They split up about a year ago but still see each other at least once a week and, occasionally, the three of us go out together. The problem is that I've now fallen for him. He's not my normal type but I really wouldn't mind a casual fling with him although I know it won't lead anywhere. But, I know that Annie is still very keen on him and I don't want to upset her. What do you think I ought to do?

You say that Annie and Dave split up a year ago, yet they continue to meet frequently and that Annie is still keen on Dave. My guess is that Dave is still keen on Annie! Perhaps their relationship has changed in some ways, over the last year, but it's certainly not my idea of a separation. Frankly, I feel that you should leave them to it and look elsewhere for a boyfriend. Even if a fling with Dave was on offer ... and I'm not sure that it is ... would it be worth the risk of losing a good friendship with Annie? I doubt it.

★

This girl at school has asked me out once or twice and I don't know what to say to her. She seems nice but I am not ready to go out with girls yet. Please help me.

Tell her precisely what you've told me ... that you like her but are not ready to go out with girls yet and would prefer to remain friends for the time being. And remember to be as pleasant as you possibly can! She's no doubt plucked up a lot of courage to ask you out in the first place. It wouldn't do to dampen down her bold spirit.

★

I am very jealous of my mother and I am very bothered by the fact that whenever my boyfriend comes to see me, he seems to spend hours talking to my mother and not to me. Do you think they can be in love? My mother and I live alone. She is 39 and I am 17.

Try not to turn your relationship with your mother into a competition – it's not, or shouldn't be. Your boyfriend may enjoy talking to her because she is older and mature and I would guess he doesn't have many older people to talk to who are willing to listen and take him seriously. Maybe he is learning a lot from your mother and so could you. Talk to her, tell her your fears and you will probably find they are groundless. Perhaps she is lonely. Begin to see her as an ally and not a rival and you will be surprised at the difference it makes.

★

I tried dope because my friends like it and now they're into dropping acid. I don't know whether to join them or not. They're really hassling me.

Although you may feel like following the crowd and experimenting further with acid, this is one time when you should really think about yourself and what YOU want. Acid can produce a state of hallucination which can be both horrific and dangerous. Bad trips produce depression, dizzy spells and panic attacks and some people have even committed suicide during hallucinations. Make sure that you pass on this information to your friends and tell them that you have better things to do in your free time. If they can't accept your decision and continue to hassle you, you might be well advised to think about socialising with a different set.

★

My mother has just found out that I had an abortion three months ago. I didn't tell her. I am 18 and live at home. The thing is that, since she has found out, she is making my life hell and keeps telling me I have committed murder. I was upset when I had the abortion and am very depressed by my mother's behaviour. Please advise me as I can't carry on living in this terrible atmosphere.

Your mother may be reacting so strongly because she is upset that you didn't confide in her when you were pregnant. Try to explain your reasons for having the abortion and why you did not want to worry her at the time. Tell her it had to be your decision, and yours alone, because you were the one who would have had to take responsibility for the baby. Abortion is a very difficult decision and a deeply personal one. I hope that, in time, your mother will respect the choice you made. You might find it helpful to talk through your experience with others and I suggest you contact the Women's Reproductive Rights Information Centre for info on counselling groups for women who have had an abortion.

★

I am 15 and babysit for a 5 year old boy once a week. The boy's father is a single parent and 3 months ago we started having sex regularly. I do enjoy it but feel it's wrong. Does this sound odd? Do you think I should stop doing it?

It's not odd that you feel it is wrong. For one thing, you are under the age of consent and this man must know he is breaking the law. It, therefore, has to be a secret and probably feels furtive. No doubt, you feel flattered and excited by a new adventure but you'll find it hard to deal with the emotional aftermath. I think that you ought to trust your feelings and put a stop to this relationship now. You know it is wrong. Babysit for someone else. Incidentally, I hope you've been using a contraceptive because, even though you are too young for sex in the eyes of the law, you are not too young to get pregnant and could very easily do so.

★

Please could you tell me how to stop feeling so possessive and jealous whenever I see my boyfriend talking to other females? He has been unfaithful to me in the past but I know that he loves me. I never seem to believe him when he tells me things. Sometimes I phone him and when he picks up the phone, I put it down, just to check up on him. I have been going out with him for 14 months. He is 24 and I am 18 in a couple of months. We often have arguments about this.

It doesn't sound to me like you are suffering from obsessive jealousy but that there are well founded reasons for the feelings that you are experiencing. Your boyfriend has been unfaithful in the past which has led to your current insecurity and anxiety that he might repeat his former behaviour. Perhaps the time has come for a calm and honest discussion on the subject. You cannot and should not want to prevent him from talking to other women but you can ask him for a commitment to you and your relationship with him. If he is not prepared to reassure you that his intentions are honourable, maybe you need to rethink your relationship with him. He may well say that he loves you but what are his actions saying?

★

My parents don't like me to go out with my boyfriend in his car because he drinks and drives. How can I make them see that I'm perfectly safe with him? I'm 17.

Sorry, but I have to say that I fully sympathise with your parents' point of view. Your boyfriend may well appear to be a careful driver but appearances are deceptive. Experts have found that even one drink can impair judgement. Given the potentially dangerous situation, I strongly believe that you ought to heed the words of your parents and refuse to drive with your boyfriend if he's been drinking. If he won't agree to change his ways, he is being extremely irresponsible and you might be forced to rethink your relationship with him.

★

I am a boy dying of lust for a girl. Now, this may not sound like a problem to you but it is, because my best friend always gets in the way. If I'm anywhere near her he immediately joins us. If she asks a question, he always answers. I want to be friendly with both of them. What shall I do?

Come now, surely your friend is not with you every single minute of the day and night? There must be times when he goes to the loo, visits his grandma or whatever. Wait for one of these occasions and move in on your lusted one. Ask her out and arrange a secret meeting. And I mean secret. Don't tell your friend unless you want the pleasure of his company, too. if this plan doesn't suit you, then ring her or restore the art of letter writing, never forgetting that mum's the word. If all goes well but your friend still hangs around, tell him outright that a certain degree of privacy would not go amiss.

★

My dad never gave me any sex education. One day he just called me in and said: 'I'm going to tell you about the birds and the bees. You know what people do. Well, the birds and the bees do it too'. End of conversation. I am now 16 and don't know anything very much about people, the birds or the bees! Can you please suggest some reading material. I would be most grateful.

Most certainly. For starters, I'd suggest you look at *First Love, First Sex* by Kaye Wellings and *Make it Happy and Safe* by Jane Cousins - and, once you've read them, you might like to think about lending them to your dad!

★

I'm 14 years of age and I'm scared of girls. I tend to be walked all over but there's nothing I can do. I also seem to blush a lot and can't talk out in class for fear of people looking at me. Is this a phobia of girls?

No, you are not suffering from girl phobia. Adolescence is a crisis period for many so it's not surprising that you feel vulnerable and insecure. Try and come to terms with the fact that girls are mere mortals and, like yourself, they have their problems too. Talk to those with whom you have something in common and, if you get stuck for conversation, then ask questions. People love to chat about themselves. And develop your own interests. As you become more accepting of yourself, you'll become more confident and your anxieties will fade. Good luck and keep me posted.

★

I'm 15 and my parents are really messing up my social life. They let my boyfriend visit me at home but they don't like us going out together alone. How can I change this and make them see I'm no longer a baby? I've talked to them but it makes no difference.

Given the number of letters that I receive from teenagers, it would appear that parents can seriously damage your love life. Try to look at it from their point of view. It's not easy adapting to the fact that your daughter is no longer a little girl but is on the road to independence. What's more, your parents probably remember all the awful things that they got up to as teenagers and are scared stiff that you might follow suit! But it is a positive sign that you are allowed to invite your boyfriend to your home and it's possible that, as they get to know and trust him, they may allow you more freedom. Do keep talking to them about the subject - you may reach a compromise.

★

I'm 17 and my boyfriend is beginning to make me sick. He's not very caring. He always insults me and we don't get on any more. I don't really want to go out with him but I'm scared to give him up in case I'll never have another boyfriend again. Do you think I'm being silly?

No. I don't think that you are being silly but I do think that you are selling yourself short. If your boyfriend is making you sick, could it be that you've settled for a chocolate bar when you were wanting a big roast dinner? Why not spend time with your friends and concentrate on pursuing your own interests? You won't be alone for ever, I can assure you. Just make certain that, next time around, you develop a friendship with someone who deserves you and is not going to knock your self-esteem.

★

I have a girlfriend who wants to have sex with me but I keep putting her off. I do not want to have sex at my age. Soon I will lose her if I don't do it. Please help.

Maybe you will lose her if you don't do it but, if you do do it, you will lose your virginity and I don't get the impression that that's what you want to do right now. And why should you? It would be extremely unwise to enter into a sexual relationship with her when you feel you are not ready to do so. Rather than just 'putting her off', make sure that you give your girlfriend a clear explanation of where you're at, at the moment. She may come to appreciate your understandable caution. If she doesn't, then you might be better off waiting for a kindred spirit to show up.

★

I'm 15 and have been going out with this girl for a year on and off. We had sex last Tuesday for the first time with no contraception (an impulse). Now I want to know whether she may be pregnant. I didn't quite ejaculate but I know that it could leak out. She is also 15. Please help.

There is a risk of pregnancy, even if you did not ejaculate fully. It's a small risk and I can only hope, as I'm sure you do, that your girlfriend is not pregnant. Impulses of this kind can be dangerous. The next time that you decide to have sex, make sure that you act responsibly and take contraceptive precautions. And do please bear in mind that it's illegal to have sex with a girl who is under the age of 16.

★

This might sound silly but, at 18 I can't seem to find my clitoris. Can you tell me where it is?

This doesn't sound silly at all. Lots of women are unfamiliar with their genital area which is somewhat discreetly tucked away unlike the 'let it all hang out' male version. The clitoris is the small knob of tissue at the front of the vulva. It's partly covered by a fold of skin called the clitoral hood which is analogous to the male foreskin. As you'd like to get to know yourself more intimately, why not give yourself a guided tour of your genital area? Your own body, a good diagram of the female anatomy, a small mirror and a torch is all that's needed.

★

My problem is that I've not had sex before and wondered how I can get rid of my anxiety. I freeze up whenever my boyfriend tries to enter me. He is very loving and considerate. Even if the right time comes and I'm ready for it, I'm frightened that something might go wrong.

It's possible that you are 'freezing up' because you don't yet feel ready for sexual intercourse. Think about it. Do you want to have sex with your boyfriend or are you merely trying to please him? If the latter is the case, then you are probably suffering from some degree of stage-fright – perfectly natural when you've not had intercourse before. Try and set aside some time to explore your body on your own, before attempting intercourse again. Buy some KY Jelly. Put a little on a finger and insert it into the vagina, gently moving it around. Repeat this exercise a few times a week. Once you are more comfortable with your own body, you'll be less likely to 'freeze' with your boyfriend.

★

I am an 18 year old male virgin. I have been dating a girl for 3 years now and she will not make love with me. She says 'it's not right now'. We've been alone plenty of times together and she will not respond to sex. Kissing and cuddling yes, but intercourse no. I have never applied pressure. What is wrong? Thank you.

I don't see that there is anything wrong. There is an awful lot of emphasis on sex these days but I don't believe that anyone should enter into a sexual relationship until they are ready to do so. Your girlfriend is happy to kiss and cuddle but is not ready for sexual intercourse. That sounds perfectly reasonable to me. Are you perhaps concerned that at 18 you should no longer be a virgin? For, in this day and age, virginity is becoming very fashionable and could even be said to be an advantage! It's good that you have not applied any pressure on your girlfriend. You risk losing her if you do.

★

My girlfriend and I have started having sex. It's the first sexual relationship for both of us and it's great except that I'm a premature ejaculator. Can you help with my problem?

Please believe me when I say that men with amazing ejaculatory control don't grow on trees. At the start of their sexual careers, most young chaps tend to climax rapidly but, in a good relationship and with a bit of practice, soon pick up the techniques for delaying ejaculation. Have a look at *Men and Sex* by Bernie Zilbergeld, if you fancy a little reading matter on the subject. But above all, don't worry and remember that 'Sandra says Relax.' You do not have a problem but are merely learning the tricks of the trade!

★

We are two teenage girls, deeply depressed, half way up a motorway. Our mother has pushed us on a coach with a whole load of strangers and we are heading for Devon for two weeks. We miss our Grandmother's cooking. We miss everything except our mother's cooking. She's so busy, she only has time to give us the occasional bowl of gruel. Help! (Two Sting fans half way up a motorway.)

Do you honestly think I'm that daft that I can't recognise a letter from my two delightful daughters! Now, watch it girls. Are you trying to ruin my professional reputation? I did not push you on a coach. You went willingly with a few words of encouragement. As for the bowls of gruel ... are you not forgetting the cordon bleu cornflakes? Have a wonderful time and don't worry about me. While the Sting fans are away, the Agony Aunt can play!

6

Turn-Offs

Unaccustomed as I am to being sexist, the letters that you are about to read are, in the main, from women! I did try my best to redress the balance but to no avail. It would appear that my female readers are far more perturbed about their partners' peccadilloes than vice versa.

This could indicate one of numerous things. Perhaps women are the fussier sex. Perhaps men don't like to complain in public. Perhaps my mailbag is not indicative of society at large. Or could it simply be that, overall, women's ways are less offensive than those of the male? Without wishing to alienate half of my readership I'm inclined to believe the latter.

But let's hope I'm wrong! I have no desire whatsoever to be left with an image of millions of well-scrubbed women who don't pick their spots or fart in bed, having to tolerate the tortuous turn-offs emanating from their nearest and dearest.

Tune in for turn-offs.

★

This window-cleaner and I have been going out together for a few weeks. He's very clever and has a degree in sociology. Three days ago we arranged to go to the cinema and planned to meet in a restaurant for a meal beforehand. The problem is that he never showed up. Neither did he telephone and he hasn't telephoned since. I don't understand it. We were getting on so well. Should I telephone him or just forget all about it?

While some of my best friends are window cleaners with sociology degrees, I don't think it follows that they are all very clever. Your chap doesn't sound too clever to me. He's had three days to ring in with a plausible explanation, yet you've not heard a word. If I were you, I wouldn't bother making contact with him – plod on with the rest of life and try to put him to one side. We can, of course, revise our opinion of him if you suddenly hear that he's dropped off his ladder and passes the time of day dreaming about you in a hospital bed!

★

My boyfriend makes funny squeaking noises when we make love and it gets on my nerves. How can I get him to stop?

You could playfully suggest you would be more excited by a deep-throated roar and ask him to experiment with noises. Join him in the experiment and see what sort of noises you can make together. Love-making is rarely silent. If the people aint squeaking, the bed is creaking. So relax and enjoy the idiosyncracies.

★

My boyfriend told me the other day that he has a secret urge to be a flasher. I was appalled. Should I end our affair?

Whether you end your affair or not depends entirely on how much you feel for your boyfriend. His telling you about his urge to be a flasher may well be a cry for help, and perhaps he needs to talk to someone who will not condemn him in order to sort himself out. It must have been a shock for you. It's certainly not easy imagining someone you love indulging in behaviour which you find repulsive, but if your relationship is one of value, try a little understanding and see if you can help him. If you cannot or don't want to do this, please suggest to him that he seek sexual counselling or psychiatric help.

★

My boyfriend is constantly picking his nose. It's really disgusting. How can I get him to stop?

Well, you could try picking yours too, preferably over dinner, and watch his reaction very closely. He may be delighted to have you join him in his habit, or be as disgusted as you are. If the latter you have proved your point and end of problem. If the former, then you may have no alternative but to say it was a relationship with a man you wanted and not a snotty nosed kid.

★

My husband is a rock'n'roll freak and, whenever we make love, he insists on playing really loud music. It's driving me mad and turning me off sex completely. He says that he finds the music very romantic but I find it a real turn off. Do you have any advice on this matter? Thanks.

Your husband obviously thinks that rock'n'roll is the food of love. What he has to understand is that it is for some but not for others. What music makes you feel sexy? I would suggest that you arrange to make love to your music sometimes and his on others – that way you can both have fun. He can't expect to call the tune on every single occasion. Love is a matter of caring what the other person wants and we all have to make compromises and adjustments in order to build good, satisfying relationships. So, sort out some of your tapes, some of his, head for the sheets and face the music together!

★

My boyfriend is very mean with money. Whenever we go out, he always expects me to pay for everything. He is costing me a fortune which I can't afford. Should I tell him this or just go on paying? I don't want to have an argument with him and am scared that he might leave me.

I am sure there are more worthwhile ways of spending your money than on a Scrooge of a boyfriend. Explain to him that you can no longer afford to keep him in the manner to which he has become accustomed ...and if he doesn't see sense immediately, I'd give him the big elbow, if I were you. Meanness is not a pleasant trait and, if he is mean with money, my guess would be that he is mean in other ways too. Think about pampering yourself for a change and, if he doesn't shape up, start looking for a new friend who values you for yourself and not for your wallet.

★

I'm having a relationship with a mountain climber. The problem is that he spends all his holidays mounting virgin peaks and I'm dead lucky if I get to have a weekend in Hastings with him. This year I really want a good holiday on a hot beach somewhere but he's insisting that he's flying solo (well, with his climbing friends – not me) to the Himalayas. Help! What am I going to do?

Look, in the normal way, I'd say ... sit down with the gentleman concerned and don't stand up 'til you reach a compromise. But frankly, in view of the fact that you are dealing with a man with an over-climbing interest, my feeling is that you did remarkably well to reach Hastings for the weekend. I don't like to be negative but, realistically speaking, there's no way that your boyfriend is going to sacrifice his karabiners, bivvy bags and all, for a fortnight in Majorca. You have to weigh up the pros and cons as they stand. Is your relationship throughout the rest of the year worth hanging on to? If so, perhaps a separate vacation is a small price to pay for an enriching liaison during off-peak periods. Or do you spend those periods neglecting your own needs in order to nurse frost-bitten toes? Are his crampons cramping your style? Do you need to review your complete partnership?

I am 22 and very confused. I have had a sexual relationship for the past three months and have not yet had an orgasm. My boyfriend suggested we watch dirty videos to help turn me on. Do you think this will help in any way? Or is there something wrong with me?

I'm an old fashioned Sex Therapist and I'm not of the opinion that dirty videos are suddenly going to get your orgasmic reflex flexing. To my mind, such movies do not help in cases like this and can be a real turn-off depending, as they often do, on the exploitation and abuse of women. Tell your boyfriend that, if he wants to assist in turning you on, he should get his finger out and tenderly tickle your clitoris. And please don't forget that magical four-lettered word – LOVE. It's a jolly good ingredient when it comes to making successful sexual recipes.

I've been sleeping with my boyfriend for the last three months. The trouble is that, although he washes frequently, he doesn't take many baths and his penis smells. Otherwise, I am very fond of him. What can I do?

Unfortunately, there are people who seem to be of the opinion that what doesn't normally show, doesn't need washing. Whereas they may be fastidious about keeping their faces clean, they do not pay the same attention to other parts of the body. Lack of genital hygiene is obviously unhealthy as well as being a sexual turn-off. I can't see that you have any choice but to be direct with your boyfriend and, as tactfully as you can, remind him that 'cleanliness is next to godliness!' If you make it quite clear that it is no longer divine to be with him, he will, I hope, think about making a clean slate.

My sex life is awful. It's all because my wife spends her life glued to the television watching soap operas. I can't seem to distract her. Can you think

of anything drastic that I could do to pep up our marriage?

I'm not sure that drastic measures are going to go down too well with your wife. If you were to turn off the television with a view to turning her on instead, you could find yourself face to face with the Wild Woman of Wonga. No-one but no-one reacts kindly to having their daily fix taken away without their consent. Best to approach the situation with caution initially and see what ensues. There's a good hour and a half going free in between 'Neighbours' and 'East Enders'. Use this time constructively to woo your wife away from the likes of Scott, Dirty Den et al. It might mean that you'll be obliged to sacrifice the Six o'Clock News for a while but that's the price you'll have to pay for working at your marriage. Can't wait to hear how you get on. Don't forget to let me know!

★

My sex life is suffering because my wife can't stand the smell of smoke on my breath and I can't give up smoking. We have been married for ten years and it has always been a problem. My wife says that if I can stop we will lead a normal sex life. Help!

If you and your wife haven't managed to reach a compromise over the last 10 years, I doubt that you'll do so now. Hence – it looks like the time has come for your to take your pick. Do you want to have a smokeless, normal sex life or would you prefer to be a smoking celibate? Your choice. I can only remind you that sex is still a relatively healthy activity if you stick to one partner. Smoking, however, kills 200 people a day in England and Wales.

★

My boyfriend used to take the occasional amphetamine tablet but lately he seems to take more and more. What can I do to stop him?

One of the main problems associated with amphetamines (also known as speed) is that, in order to get the desired effect, one must continually increase the dosage. This is presumably what your boyfriend is doing but, as I've said countless times before, he won't stop taking the tablets unless he chooses to do so. All you can do is emphasise that heavy use of amphetamines is extremely dangerous and suggest that he seek help as quickly as possible. He could contact Narcotics Anonymous or write to SCODA, for assistance.

My boyfriend has some pretty revolting habits. All my friends say that I'll be able to change him after we are married. What do you think?

I think it was Natalie Wood who said that the only time you can change a man is when he's wearing a nappy. Frankly, I'm inclined to believe this and feel that your friends are being over optimistic! Now, I don't know what your boyfriend's revolting habits are, but, nevertheless, I would strongly suggest that you only consider going ahead with the wedding if you can tolerate him as he is. Any attempt to mould him into your image of the ideal husband would be a sure recipe for disaster, in my humble opinion. It's your decision, of course.

★

My husband and I have been married for ten years. We got on very well until a couple of years ago when my husband started to gamble. Things have gone from bad to worse, and he has even started borrowing money, solely for the purpose of gambling. I just don't know how to handle this situation and am at my wits' end. How can I make him stop, since it is ruining our marriage?

Living with a compulsive gambler, like living with anyone with an addiction, does put enormous pressures on a relationship and I'm not surprised to hear that you are at your wits' end. Speak with your husband and find out whether he would be willing to seek help. If he wants to stop gambling — in reality, I don't think that you can make him stop — tell him to contact Gamblers Anonymous, an organisation which runs support groups throughout the country. You may wish to get in touch with Gam Anon, for the relatives of compulsive gamblers. Ring the same number for further details.

★

I'm fed up with my husband's heavy drinking habits. He says that he doesn't have a drink problem because he never touches spirits. But he drinks gallons of beer and, apart from anything else, it's having a disastrous effect on our sex life. Any advice?

Getting other people to give up their horrible habits is no easy business. Certainly, I think you ought to inform your husband that a pint of beer has the same alcoholic content as a double whisky. You can also give him the phone number of Alcoholics Anonymous. The rest is up to him. Drinking in excess creates all sorts of difficulties as, I'm afraid, you are beginning to experience. If you yourself would like to seek help, contact Al Anon – an organisation which runs local support groups for the relatives and friends of problem drinkers.

★

My wife and I love each other but she won't tolerate me as I am and hates my drinking and smoking habits. I've always been a heavy drinker and smoker and my wife seemed to accept this until a couple of years ago when she started to nag me. I can't take the tension. The more she nags, the more I smoke and drink. Can you give me any advice?

In theory, love is all about tolerance, but, in practice, no-one likes to watch the person they love destroy her/him self and your wife's reactions are understandable. Perhaps she also feels that she alone ought to be able to satisfy your oral needs! People tend not to give up long term addictions, however, just because someone asks them to do so. Explain to your wife that nagging is, if anything, making the situation worse. If you want to change your ways, counselling might help. If you don't, you don't and both you and your wife will have no choice but to accept the consequences. Good luck.

★

I tend to sweat a lot although I am of medium build and 36. This has been a problem with me since my teens. I did see the doctor but all he could suggest was wash more often which I already do a lot. I have a bath every day and use anti-perspirant but it's not enough. I am quite hairy and hot-blooded but still find my sweating an embarrassment. Can you help a neurotic male?

The smell of fresh sweat is not unpleasant; in fact lots of women find it very appealing. It's the stale sweat on long-unwashed bodies that is a real turn-off. Continue your daily baths and anti-perspirant and try a dusting of talcum powder too. The other thing you can do is make sure all your clothes are always freshly laundered or cleaned so that they do not carry the odour of over active armpits! Some people do sweat more than others, it's the way they are made. If you keep your personal hygiene up to the very highest standards, I don't think you'll have anything to worry about.

★

Ever since my wife had a baby she's paid me no attention at all. The other day I kicked a hole in the kitchen wall and she didn't even look up to see what was going on. Please can you advise?

If the behaviour that you describe is typical of your behaviour in general, do you honestly think it's surprising that your wife has grown unaccustomed to your ways? Sorry to be so pessimistic but it sounds to me like you were merely a substitute infant until the real thing came along. If it's not too late to resurrect your marriage, I would say that you only have one option open to you. Like it or not, my friend, it's time to grow up. Therapy could help but it's a lengthy process. You need to make a few changes today if you still want to be in with a chance. Perhaps you could start by talking with your wife instead of wasting energy destroying the happy home.

★

Please help us. Our boss has very smelly BO and we nearly suffocate every day. How do we tell him?

There is no kind way to tell someone that he smells bad, and the chances are he won't believe you anyway. If his own nose hasn't told him by now, he won't be inclined to trust yours. As you are finding it unbearable, however, you are going to have to be brave and broach the subject firmly but politely. It might provoke a storm but, on the other hand, if he has been unaware of the problem, he may be grateful that you've raised this delicate matter and put him on the road to clean living.

★

My boyfriend suffers from greasy hair. I've tried hinting he wash it more but it doesn't seem to work. What can I do? I am desperate.

If your boyfriend has not responded to your gentle hints, the time for hints is over. Tell him straight out that his greasy hair is a real turn off. Next, direct him to the nearest shampoo selling shop and, finally, lock him up, lock, stock and barrel, in the nearest bathroom until he's done the dirty deed. This should do the trick. Sadly, grease-proof guys do not exist but, if a chap wants to keep a girlfriend, he's got to make efforts to clean up his act.

★

I've never liked my daughter-in-law very much and strongly disapprove of her methods of bringing up children. She seems far too casual, doesn't seem to pay any attention to their eating habits and lets them watch too much television. I have occasionally discussed this with my son but he's always told me to mind my own business. What do you think I should do?

I think you should heed your son's words and let them bring up the children their way. I realise that this is tough advice to follow, but if you interfere you will only cause yourself more pain. Being a mother-in-law is a difficult business and has to be carried out with tact and delicacy. If your son and his wife are aware that you don't like her, then they will resent even more any criticism you make of their child rearing methods. Try to maintain a certain detachment, and just enjoy your grand-children from the happy position of not having to be responsible for bringing them up.

★

My girlfriend sometimes takes cocaine. She says it makes her feel really sexy and that I ought to try it. What do you think?

I think that you would be crazy to start taking cocaine. It's a drug which is far more likely to damage your sex life, not to mention your health, than improve it. Your girlfriend may well find the short-term effects of cocaine exciting but, in the long-term, these good feelings will certainly be replaced by sickness, restlessness, weight loss, depression and fatigue. High doses can sometimes cause death from breathing failure or heart attack ... none of which is going to improve your sex life, is it now?

★

My husband and I have been married for three years. Everything was fine until three months ago when our first child was born. Since this time he has been acting like a spoilt child and seems to get very jealous of the baby. He keeps complaining that I show him no affection and that I've stopped loving him. This isn't the case at all but obviously I have to give a lot of attention to the baby and things can't be the same as before. I'm feeling very tired and fed up with my husband even though I do still love him. How can I make things change for the better and get him to grow up?

Talk to your husband while the baby is asleep. He is obviously finding parenthood a hard adjustment and may not realise how unreasonable he is being. The birth of a child is high on the stress list. Not only does it alter the balance of a relationship, but it is also a reminder of our own childhoods and can bring up memories and anxieties long buried and forgotten. Maybe he does resent the baby, but can't say so, and is resenting you instead. If you could share your feelings it would help. Sharing the baby would, of course, be even better!

★

My boyfriend always insists on smoking cannabis when he comes to visit me at my flat. I really don't like drugs and don't want him to do this but he won't take me seriously. What should I do?

Apart from the fact that you don't like your boyfriend smoking in your flat, I ought to mention that it is an offence to allow anyone on your premises to smoke cannabis. If he wants to take the risk in his own place, then that's his decision but it's not fair to insist on smoking at your flat when you obviously don't want him to do so. If he's not prepared to take your request seriously, I can only suggest that you take a firm line and tell him that he can't visit you any longer. When he sees that you mean business he might consider changing his ways.

★

Do you think that love conquers all? I love my boyfriend very much but we have severe problems because he is so possessive and aggressive. He wants me to marry him but I don't know if my love for him will be enough. Please help as I am very worried.

No, I don't think love conquers all. It might for a short time, but being the object of someone's possessive and aggressive feelings for year after year will soon put paid to any affection. It may be flattering that someone is so possessive about you now but it will become irksome and unpleasant over a long period. Think very carefully before you embark upon marriage with this man. Unless you believe that he is likely to change his attitude and become more mature and loving, then I would advise you not to commit yourself to a lifetime with him.

7
Masturbation

'Don't knock masturbation. It's sex with someone I love,' said Woody to Diane in *Annie Hall*.

Not a lot more to say really, is there?

My wife told me the other day that sometimes, if I'm away on a business trip, she masturbates using a vibrator and fantasises that she's with me. I must say that I was quite flattered but wondered what you felt. Do you think this is a problem?

Not at all. Your wife is enjoying herself and you feel flattered. No problem! Just let me give you a few words of warning, however. A friend of mine recently told me that she finds her vibrator more emotional that her husband. Make sure you treat your wife well when you are around!

★

When I was in America on holiday, I saw a blue movie and this man was masturbating whilst in a very complicated yoga position. I've been trying to do the same thing with no success. Do you have any suggestions?

I'm afraid I haven't! You and I obviously don't share the same taste in films and I've not seen or heard of this one. All sounds very strange to me. Yoga and masturbation hardly go together like peaches and cream. I would only advise that you don't force your body to do what doesn't come naturally. Perhaps, for you, this is 'position impossible!'

★

At the age of 24, I continually have the urge to masturbate. Despite being happily married, every time I look at myself in the bathroom mirror, I just cannot stop myself. Am I abnormal? Please help.

Do you remember the story about Narcissus? He was the beautiful youth who was so besotted by his own reflection in a fountain that he gradually pined away until he was transformed into the flower that bears his name. What I'm trying to say is that there ain't nothing wrong with doing a bit of DIY in the bathroom. But it worries me that you spend so much time looking at yourself in the mirror. Do you want to turn into a flower or would you rather continue to be a happily married geyser? The choice is yours. You can open the box or take the money!

★

My three year old daughter often masturbates. Is this normal?

Yes, it is normal. Lots of small children masturbate. It's important your daughter is not made to feel it is wrong and guilty because this will inhibit her in later life. If, however, she has a vaginal discharge, soreness or itching in the genital area, take her to your GP because this is not normal and you need medical advice.

★

I think I may be perverted because I read adult mags and I frequently masturbate to the pictures in them. Please help me.

Some people masturbate several times a day; others do so once a year. But, whatever the frequency, masturbation is a perfectly harmless activity and does not make you go blind, insane or cause hair to grow on the palms of your hands! Masturbation is usually accompanied by fantasies and whether you choose to look at adult mags or create your own sexual images is up to you. Providing that you confine yourself to the privacy of your own room, there is no way that anyone could consider you to be a pervert.

★

I have a terrible problem. I seem to get a kick out of masturbating when there is a danger of being caught, like in the dentist's waiting room. Please help.

Whilst there is nothing wrong with masturbation, to do so in public is asking for trouble. Indecent exposure is a crime and, if you carry on in this way, you could well end up being reported to the police and convicted. This type of behaviour is often a form of attention seeking and indicates that an individual might have problems in relating to other people. I think that you would do well to seek counselling help and examine why you have the need to act in this way. Ask your GP to refer you to a counsellor or contact IDENTITY.

★

I am a 33 year old woman. My boyfriend and I split up about six months ago, and, although I've come to terms with the end of the affair, I really miss not having a sex life. I've had a number of sexual propositions but I haven't felt that I wanted to have sex with any of the proposers! I'd rather hang on until I meet someone that I really care about. Meanwhile, for the first time in my life, I have taken to masturbating regularly. Do you think that this will do me any harm?

No, I don't. Despite the fact that many people today still believe that masturbation causes insanity, blindness, sterility and so on, this is not the case. Most people masturbate sometimes, even when they do have a sexual partner. You've made a perfectly reasonable decision not to enter into a sexual relationship until you meet someone whom you consider to be special. Don't feel guilty about masturbating. It is a valid and healthy form of sexual expression.

★

Even though my husband and I have a full and active sex life, he still masturbates from time to time. This doesn't really bother me but I'm not sure that it's natural. Should I encourage him to see a doctor?

No – this is not a 'problem' requiring medical attention. It is perfectly normal and the only reason for asking your husband not to do it would be if it really upset you and made you unhappy. Since you say that this is not the case, I don't see that anything needs to be done at all.

★

I often feel the desire to dress up in my mother's underwear and masturbate. Please help.

If my mail bag is anything to go by, it would appear that there are lots of chaps out there who get turned on by wearing female underwear. Chacun à son goût, I always say. But I also have to say that I have mixed feelings about you wearing your mother's underwear. She's not really the best person to have an affair with, even in fantasy. Could you not save up some money and buy your own pair of knickers?

★

Help! I'm only 13 and I always think about girls and masturbate at least one or two times a day. Is this normal and safe?

I receive numerous letters, from people of all ages, concerned about the fact that they masturbate. So, let me say, once and for all, that masturbation is a perfectly normal and safe activity. Most people do it sometimes. Some people do it several times a day; others once in a blue moon. The only danger from masturbation is that, if you really get hooked on it and masturbate at every available opportunity, you'll find that there won't be any time left to do your homework!

★

I've never had sex with anyone but there is one thing that is truly bothering me. Could I get AIDS from masturbating? I masturbate a lot.

There is no AIDS risk attached to solo masturbation so relax and enjoy it. If you'd like to learn more about AIDS, remember that you can always write to the Terence Higgins Trust, for some of their excellent leaflets on the subject.

★

I am 18 years old and a virgin. This is not my problem but what I'm worried about is the fact that I masturbate at least once a day and I feel this must be harmful to me. I fantasise about every girl I meet. I am worried that the size of my penis may have been hindered by this. Also, when I climax, I only release enough spunk to fill a soup spoon. Please help.

Masturbation rules OK, OK? And do not fear – it will not affect the size of your penis. Fantasising is fine too. As for the amount of ejaculate you release when you climax ... please heed my words when I say that a soup spoon of spunk is not to be sneezed at. Be it enough to fill a soup spoon or a ladle is of no importance whatsoever.

★

I can't stop masturbating. I'm a 24 year old girl and I masturbate at least six times day. Do you think I am mentally ill?

I don't think that you are mentally ill because you masturbate six times a day. But I do think it's possible that you are suffering from a considerable amount of anxiety. It's often the case that people who masturbate compulsively use masturbation as a way of calming themselves down. It's probably a lot healthier than taking tranquillisers! If I'm right and you do have unresolved problems which are making you anxious – think about talking them through with a counsellor.

★

I am a 17 year old girl currently seeing a 27 year old man. When we have sex I get no pleasure at all and because of this I have been with five other men before I met him. I am not proud of myself. I was just looking for the man who would satisfy me. So far no-one has managed it. When I masturbate it is fantastic and I orgasm greatly but I never feel a thing when with a man. Is there something wrong with me?

Look, leaping into the sack with every available man in the hope that one of them will be able to give you that elusive orgasm is crazy. There is much more to sex than the mere mechanics of it.
You are only 17. Why not continue to enjoy yourself on your own, as you clearly do, until you meet someone with whom you can have a more rounded relationship? And don't forget that you can always contact a counsellor at your local Brook Advisory Centre, if you'd like to talk about this problem further.

★

I am circumcised and my favourite pastime is masturbating. I do it several times a day and, when I have the time, I spend one or two hours doing it while looking at magazines. I know how to control my ejaculations to get maximum pleasure. Nonetheless, I usually end up with sores on the left side of the head of the penis. I am left-handed. Could this have something to do with the sores?

Most probably. Bear in mind that the skin of your hand, be it left or right, is considerably rougher than the sensitive tissues of the penis. Coupled with this, you are giving yourself a lot of friction over a long period of time. In the normal way, I don't advise people to stop masturbating but, in your case, it sounds as if you need to give your penis a break and allow it to heal up. See your GP for further advice on this subject. Finally, may I suggest that you find a new pastime, if only temporarily, which would also involve the use of your hands. Could knitting, for example, be the answer? I leave the decision to you.

★

I am 17 years old and male. I have not yet had a steady girlfriend and do not look old enough to get into pubs like my mates. At the moment I have to arouse myself and think about people who I see at work or are on television. I do it nearly every night now. What should I do?

I know you won't want to hear this, but you have years and years ahead of you in which to have steady girlfriends and to give the brewers your hard-earned cash. There's more to life than pubs and sex ... that's what I think anyway ... although I guess that some of my acquaintances would disagree with me! Use your youth and energy to enjoy all the things that lots of young people do enjoy. Take up a sport. Learn to play a musical instrument. Enrol in a dance class – or whatever turns you on. You'll make new friends along the way and will probably find that hanging round the pub doesn't have half the charm you think it has now. As for masturbation – don't worry about it!

★

I did not know until recently that females masturbated and, since a friend told me about it, I tried it. It was very enjoyable. At home no-one ever talked about sexual matters and my mother has this thing about women forgetting their private parts. The thing is that after masturbation, I feel dirty and degraded but it makes me feel good as well. Am I abnormal?

I don't know if you are asking if it's abnormal to masturbate or abnormal to feel guilty. On both accounts, however, I would suggest that you are pretty run of the mill, if you don't mind me saying so! For many centuries men and women have been told by society, the church, their parents etc. that masturbation was a despicable act. It comes as no surprise, therefore, that so many people, yourself included, feel guilty afterwards.

What you should have been taught is that your genitals are not a separate entity but part of your whole body and your body, like the marvellous machine it is, requires servicing. After all, you don't feel guilty if you have a good meal or go to the gym for a work-out, do you?

★

Not having anyone to relate to sexually, I rely on self-stimulation all the time. Thankfully, I have a great imagination, dating back to schooldays. What I find, though, is that my ejaculations are very quiet. I feel pleasure but no great orgasmic feelings. Is there a leaflet on techniques for masturbation?

No leaflet that I know about although books on the subject do exist. But I don't think that any amount of literature is going to change your 'non-orgasmic ejaculations'. I get the feeling that you are not letting yourself go and that, at the time of ejaculation, you control your feelings. Try to 'go with' the pleasurable sensations and allow the pleasure to fill your body and your mind. That way, you will become orgasmic.

★

What does 'tossing off' mean? My boyfriend, who is 17, keeps telling me that he has to 'toss off' and it's all my fault because I won't have sex with him. I'm 15.

'Tossing off' is a slang expression for masturbation. There is absolutely nothing wrong with 'tossing off' and it's far better that your boyfriend do this than have sex with you. It's not your fault that he's masturbating and, anyway, you are below the age of consent. No-one should have sex until they are ready for it. Do ensure that you make your own decisions and do not enter into a sexual liaison to please someone else.

★

I have got to know a man through a lonely hearts column. He phones me up and we both masturbate and say things to each other. We both want the same thing and have no intention of meeting. Do you think I am terrible in doing such a thing? I'm afraid that I am mentally ill for feeling this way. I'm 22 and he's a few years older than me.

There is no harm in doing what you are doing. I don't think it is a terrible thing and it does not mean that you are mentally ill. But, in view of the fact that you never intend to meet this man, your relationship with him is somewhat unreal. And it's obviously disturbing you, otherwise you would not have written to me in the first place. You may find it helpful to discuss your feelings about this situation and about relationships in general, with a counsellor.

Think about asking your GP to refer you to someone or contact the Brook Advisory Centre.

I told my girlfriend that, when I don't see her, I often think about her and masturbate. She got very upset about this, called me 'disgusting' and said she didn't want to go out any more. We haven't seen each other for three weeks. I'm really sad and want her back. What can I do?

I'm sorry your girlfriend reacted so strongly to what you told her. 'Tis a pity that she didn't take it as a compliment. There's nothing wrong with fantasising about a partner and masturbating during an absence. Why not telephone her and explain that your activity is seen as totally respectable by the 'sexperts?!' Or send her a copy of this letter and answer. She might not respond positively but you never know ...

I have masturbated regularly for some years and don't feel guilty about it. I enjoy it a lot but I always feel a little depressed afterwards. This depression doesn't last long but it worries me. Is it unusual to feel this way?

It's not unusual to feel tired or depressed after masturbating or, indeed, after sex with a partner. Let me remind you of the old Latin maxim 'Post coitum omne animal triste' (every animal is sad after coitus). You've no doubt been experiencing the joys of cloud nine and have discovered that the return journey to earth can be a trifle disconcerting. Don't worry about it, particularly as your depression is not longstanding.

I am 17 and no-one has touched my penis yet. My method of masturbating is to put a pillow under me and rub against it. I told this to a friend and he laughed at me and called me a weirdo. Am I? Could you also please tell me if masturbation stunts your growth?

No sir. You are not a weirdo. People masturbate in numerous different ways. You've selected a method which suits you and that's fine by me! And no, it will not stunt your growth. All sorts of fantastic catastrophes have been linked to the practice of masturbation. They certainly make interesting reading but have no foundation in fact.

★

Is it true that if you masturbate a lot you will become a premature ejaculator? I always come very quickly when with my girlfriend.

Masturbation in the male has been linked to premature ejaculation. As so many people were raised to believe that there was something sinful about this form of sexual expression – the main object of the exercise was to get it over and done with as quickly as possible. And I guess that, once you get into the pattern of coming quickly, it's difficult not to do the same when having sex with a partner. But, as I've said elsewhere, it's not difficult to learn how to slow down and delay ejaculation. Forgive me if I make yet another reference to *Men and Sex* by Bernie Zilbergeld but it's an excellent book and, if you read it, you should be able to pick up lots of tips on lasting longer.

8

Body Talk

From ears that stick out too much to penises that don't stick out enough, letters from readers who are dissatisfied with their bodies roll in thick and fast. It's the 'grass is always greener' syndrome. If only I looked like my best friend/Frank Bruno/Princess Di, life would take on a whole new meaning. But that's not the way it works.

Take yours truly as merely one example. An adolescent in those halcyon days of low fibre and high cholesterol, I was, perhaps, a trifle on the plump side but not unduly perplexed until Twiggy arrived on the modelling scene and got under my skin. If only I could look like her, I fantasised day after day after day, the President of the Student's Union might give me a second glance.

'Twas not to be. A diet of lettuce leaves and the many hours spent ironing away my curls, led to nothing but alopecia and a look which was hungry but not lean.

Such is life, my friends. There has to come a point in time when we learn to tolerate ourselves as we are, dimples, pimples and all.

I would like to persuade my wife to shave off her pubic hair. Do you think this is a good idea?

Well, it's your wife's body and I don't think that you ought to persuade her to do anything to it unless it appeals to her. If she's willing, then no problem. If she isn't, I feel it would be unwise to force the issue. I must say that I've never quite understood why so many people seem to prefer the bare pubis. To my mind, pubic hair is not only rather pretty but also a resource which can be put to very good use during love-making. But, enough of my thoughts! In this case, you must ask your wife for hers.

★

My boyfriend wants me to have sex with him. The problem is that he is quite overweight and, although I love him, I am frightened that he will squash me or cause me physical harm during love-making. Is this likely?

I think it's highly unlikely, especially if he follows Barbara Cartland's advice for 'real' gentlemen and uses his knees and his elbows! There are, however, lots of lovemaking positions you can use where he doesn't need to be on top and this would not only add a little variety to your love life but also relieve you of the worry that you might be injured. You could also, of course, gently urge your boyfriend to take up a sport and watch his food intake so that he will be leaner and healthier all round.

★

I only have a small penis and girls I know always laugh at me. Wha *can I do? I feel I will only disappoint girls if I sleep with them.*

Dear, oh dear. I don't mean to sound unsympathetic but I wa: hoping I'd convinced all you chaps out there that worrying about th size of your penis is a waste of good worrying time. Penises, like finger and toes, come in a variety of sizes and there is nothing you can do t change them. What's more, penis size has no bearing on sexual pleasur and desirability. Listen, my friend, whoever has been laughing at th size of your penis does not deserve the pleasure of it's company. Lov means never having to ridicule your partner's protuberances. Forg about sleeping with 'them'. Save yourself for one good woman and your confidence will be restored. Okay?

★

My husband thinks my nipples look boring and wants me to have them pierced. I'm not sure whether this is a good idea or not. I have checked it out and the man who does it uses all sterile needles and rings. Do you think I am mad to allow this?

Frankly, yes! I think that you are indeed crazy to consider this form of self-mutilation. So, if your husband were my husband, I'd tell him to stop driving me mad and go pierce his own nipples if he's got nothing better to do. Well, you did ask for my opinion, didn't you?! But I suppose I ought also to mention that it's not an opinion shared by the professional nipple piercer with whom I've just been chatting. He informs me that the piercing of the nipples is as painless and as harmless as ear piercing, if carried out properly. Your nipples - your decision!

★

I have read in a book for women that if you have hairs around the areola part of your breasts, it can be caused by hormonal changes due to pregnancy or the pill. Is this true, or can the hairs just grow anyway? It worried me after reading this even though I am not on the pill. My boyfriend uses condoms and I am quite certain that I am not pregnant.

Please stop worrying! Whilst it's true that pregnancy and the pill can sometimes affect hair growth, it's perfectly normal to have some hairs around the nipple and this does not mean that you are pregnant.

★

I have lived with one partner for the last ten years. My girlfriend, about two years ago, decided that she was overweight and, as such, feels too ugly to have a sexual relationship. I am not an aggressive person and prefer to give the situation time. I have tried to get her to have some counselling for this problem and her other problem which is depression. I wish to understand but find it difficult.

Loss of interest in sex is a common feature of depression. It's also not uncommon and perfectly understandable that someone who is unhappy with her body won't allow another person to get close to her. Your girlfriend's problems sound quite deep-rooted and I am sure that she would benefit from talking them through with a counsellor/therapist. But you can't force her to seek help if she doesn't want to. I'm glad that you are not an aggressive man. Be patient and allow your girlfriend to talk to you. Hopefully, she will come to the realisation that she has the power to change her situation.

★

Hello. I have a very personal problem. You are the only person I can turn to. My testicles are out of proportion to the rest of my body. My girlfriend always sniggers when I remove my underpants. Please help me.

You don't say in which way you think your testicles are out of proportion but my guess would be that you are no more oddly proportioned than the next man. Variations in size are the rule in these matters but you don't have to take my word for it. As you are concerned, it would probably be a good idea to arrange to see your GP and discuss your anxieties with her/him. I would also recommend that you stop removing your underpants in front of your girlfriend, certainly until she gives up the insensitive habit of sniggering.

★

My boyfriend is obsessed with rock hard stomachs. He keeps telling me that, unless I can firm up my stomach muscles, he is going to go off with my best friend. I have been doing exercises, but my stomach is the same as it ever was. I know that my best friend fancies my boyfriend and I'm really concerned. Can you help?

Anyone who threatens you with ending a relationship because you don't measure up to his idea of perfection is not worth the candle. And then to tell you that he'll run off with your best friend … sorry, but I'm so appalled that I am lost for words. If I were you, I would not give this boyfriend of yours the time of day. What I would most definitely give him is the elbow, in the stomach of course!

★

My cousin told me that she is saving up for a 'fanny-plasty'. She said it's something to do with her body but she wouldn't tell me what it is. Do you know?

I would imagine that your cousin is planning to have plastic surgery on her genitals. There are women who resort to such surgery for alterations to their anatomy because they dislike the size and shape of their labia (inner and outer lips of the vulva). The labia do vary greatly in size from female to female and it strikes me as very sad that so many women, who have perfectly normal genitals, appear to think that their bodies are deformed in some way. Why don't you suggest to your cousin that she see a Sex Therapist who might be able to help her come to terms with her body as it is? But, obviously, the final decision is hers. You can't prevent her from having plastic surgery, if that's what she really wants.

★

My penis, when erect, only measures six and a quarter inches long. Can you recommend any exercises to increase its length?

No. I can't recommend any exercises to increase the size of your penis but I would strongly recommend that you throw away your tape measure! Take it from me ... your penis is of perfectly adequate proportions, and it makes no sense to worry about its size which is determined by the wicked witch, Heredity! As Bernie Zilbergeld says in *Men and Sex* ' ... unless you are contemplating a transplant from a horse, it's the only penis you'll ever have and, whatever its characteristics, it can give you much pleasure'. If you want to read Doc Zilbergeld's book, it's in paperback and published by Fontana.

★

My girlfriend keeps complaining that my ears stick out too much. I was never very bothered by my ears but I'm developing a complex. What should I do?

You poor thing. I think that your girlfriend is being extremely cruel and that you ought not to tolerate her complaints any longer. Tell her that, if she can't learn to love you, ears and all, you'll start looking around for someone who can. And take heart from the story of Clark Gable. Warner Brothers turned him down for a role in *Little Caesar* because they didn't like his ears ... but Clark made his way in the world and so will you!

★

I am nearly 15 and I am one of the few girls I know who is still flat-chested. Do you think I am abnormal?

Most definitely not. Many physical changes take place during puberty but they don't necessarily happen at the same time for everyone. Some girls develop breasts at the age of ten whereas others are still flat-chested at sixteen or seventeen. Most adolescents, boys as well as girls, become highly sensitive about their bodies during this time of change, so it's not surprising that you are feeling a little anxious. But don't worry. There is nothing wrong with you. You are unique and will develop at your own pace.

★

My boyfriend keeps complaining about the size of my breasts and wants me to have plastic surgery to make them bigger. I was never concerned about my body before I met him, but he's made me feel very self-conscious. Would it be silly to have the operation to please him? My bust measures 34 inches.

You say that you were happy with your body until your boyfriend started to make complaints. I most certainly don't think that you should undergo surgery to please him. Your bust measurement sounds perfectly reasonable to me and, even if it were on the small side, I would still consider your boyfriend's request to be utterly unreasonable. You don't tell me how you and your boyfriend get on in other respects but I sincerely hope he's interested in more than just your bra size.

★

Whenever I have sex with my girlfriend, she complains that I don't have enough chest hair. Is it true that fondling the chest encourages the growth of hair?

Of course not. If fondling the chest were to encourage the growth of hair, then we women would have as much, if not more chest hair than you chaps! Hair growth is affected by the male hormone testosterone and no amount of fondling will make you any more shaggy than you already are. If your desire to turn into a hairy monster is overwhelming, I guess you could consider investing in a chest piece of the furred kind! But I'd suggest you tell your girlfriend that, if she wants you, she will have to accept that your chest is part of the package deal.

★

I am 13 years old and I only have a few pubic hairs. Everyone else has lots of them. When I am in the showers at school, all the boys make fun of me. Is there any way of making pubic hairs grow faster?

There is no way of making pubic hair grow faster just as there's no way of making it grow curlier, thicker, thinner etc. Your hair will grow as it grows and there's not a lot you can do about it. What you can do is your very best to ignore those silly boys who are making fun of you. Once they see that you are not affected by their stupid comments, they will stop making them.

★

I'm not very old. I'm going bald and I've read about some kind of hair cream based in pure rum, which stimulates hair growth. Do you think it works? I don't know whether to try it out or not.

There are numerous causes of hair loss and numerous products on the market claiming responsibility for new growth on old (or not so old) scalps. My hairdresser, the delightful Daniel, who knows about most things, hair and otherwise, doesn't know about hair cream based in pure rum. Daniel says: 'Perhaps this man has to come to terms with the fact that he is less hirsute than he once was.' Fair enough. I can see his point. But I can also see that, if new hair is available, you wouldn't mind a strand or two.

So, if you don't object to forking out the dosh, I guess you could try some of the cream concerned. You could also ask your GP to refer you to the NHS dermatologist, about whom I've just been reading in the papers. He's had considerable success in treating cases of hair loss. But, if all fails, think positive and read Fran Landesman's poignant poem ... 'Bums Never Get Bald'.

★

I'm 16 and don't know whether I ought to shave the hair under my arms. What is your opinion?

There's no right or wrong thing to do here – ultimately it boils down to personal taste. The vast majority of European women don't shave under their arms – it's not something they even think about. Yet there are many, no doubt influenced by women's mags etc, who find such hairs aesthetically displeasing and can't wait to get rid of them. But, as you ask for my personal opinion, I'll give it to you straight from the armpit! I don't believe that a hairy armpit makes a woman look like a Russian shotputter. I'm all in favour of hair and I don't care who knows it!

★

I am afraid I must be abnormal. My penis retracts into the body completely when not erected and I can only see the scrotum and the top of the penis's skin. This does not seem to bother the people I go with but one felt very sick recently when we undressed and now it's beginning to worry me. Do you know what is wrong?

Some people will react badly when, in the midst of sex, they discover something that they do not like. I am sure you have found partners who are put off by you wearing socks or needing a cigarette in bed. But you yourself say that previous partners were not bothered by your retracting penis. It's just bad luck that you found a person who disliked what they saw instead of enjoying what you did. I can assure you there is nothing abnormal about your genital anatomy. Next time around, try to find someone who cares about you as a whole and is seeking a real body, not a physical ideal.

★

I am an 18 year old boy and very worried about my weight. I don't eat very much but still can't seem to lose anything. I probably need to lose about half a stone. Please can you help. I'm sure that I won't find a girlfriend until I am a bit slimmer.

Losing half a stone in itself is unlikely to get you a girlfriend but it might give you that extra bit of confidence needed to ask someone out. Although you say you don't eat much, if your diet consists mainly of burgers and chips, you will end up adding more to your spare tyre. Instead, grill foods and eat plenty of fresh fruit and veg which can be just as tasty and satisying. And, don't forget the joys of regular exercise. If you'd rather look like a Californian beach boy than a beach ball (sorry, I'm getting carried away and am quite sure that you look nothing like a beach ball!) then swim, windsurf, dance, play tennis or whatever turns you on. You are bound to feel exhilarated, both physically and mentally.

★

I am 17 years old and very shy. My girlfriend wants me to make love to her but I am worried about my penis. I think my foreskin may be too tight. Before my penis becomes erect, I can retract it fully but, when it becomes erect, it won't go any further than just past the head. Also my girlfriend enjoys oral sex. Is there any harm in ejaculating in her mouth? Please help.

Your foreskin sounds perfectly fine to me but, as you are concerned, arrange to see your GP and discuss your anxieties with her/him. I'm sure you would find it reassuring to be checked over by your doctor. On reading your letter, I get the impression that it's your girlfriend who is the one who is pushing for sex and that you are trying to comply with her wishes. Whatever you do, make sure that you do not involve yourself in a sexual relationship until you feel psychologically ready to do so.

As for oral sex, there is no harm in ejaculating into your girlfriend's mouth, providing that you are both free of the HIV virus. People at risk of AIDS are advised that coming inside their partner's mouth may increase the risk.

★

My foreskin is very tight. Sometimes when I have an erection, it hurts. Several nights ago I had anal sex with another guy who was very tight and, despite the pain I felt I continued until I came. Later I noticed that I had pulled back the foreskin over the head of my penis and since then I am in total pain. I will be very embarrassed to tell my local doctor about it. My mother is his practice nurse and she does not know I am gay. Do I need to see him?

Sorry, but if your foreskin is still 'pulled back' and you are in pain, then you must see a doctor. If you can't bring yourself to visit your GP, visit your nearest casualty department. Later, when you have had treatment for your present condition, you could try doing some simple masturbatory exercises, pulling your foreskin gently a little at a time, until you have comfortably stretched it and the head of the penis is shown fully without any pain. But, first, do seek a medical opinion.

★

I am 18 years old and my penis is only 5 inches long. Because of this I find it hard to have an erection because I have no confidence. This is very sad as I used to have a great sex life when I was going out with a girl for a long time. I have no problem getting nice girls in the first place but always lose them due to sex. I enjoy female company and would love to have a great sex life as well. I am very strong emotionally but secretly need a caring girlfriend. Please advise.

Please, please believe me when I say that there's absolutely nothing wrong with the size of your penis. Neither is there anything abnormal about the fact that you don't have erections all of the time. Look, your sex life was very successful when you were in a successful relationship. It's unrealistic to expect to perform brilliantly with any Theresa, Dolores or Henrietta. You are lucky that you meet lots of nice girls. Continue to enjoy their company and don't push the sexual side of things until it seems right and mutual.

★

My girlfriend recently suggested that I have my penis pierced with a small stud. Will it cause me pain when I have sexual intercourse with her?

I've received letters in the past from potential ear, nose and nipple piercers but you are the first to write in with a penis-piercing proposition. Frankly, it's a subject that gives me the shudders and I don't even fancy investigating it. Why does your girlfriend want you to have a small stud in your penis? Is this her real desire or is she trying to tell you something?! Personally, I think you'd be crazy to have it done but, if you genuinely want to go ahead, then consult your GP first and find out the probable consequences.

Alternatively, you could send your girlfriend on her merry way and concentrate on finding a woman who is not interested in small studs. No further comment.

★

I have fallen in love with this boy I see regularly in the gym. The problem is that he works out very seriously and spends all his time admiring his own body in the mirror. How can I make him notice mine?

If you are profoundly hooked on this bloke and determined to catch his eye, I suppose you could try the 'aren't you wonderful' number. Admire his muscular frame and ask his advice on the best exercises and routines. Tell him that, give or take the odd organ, you'd like to become his female equivalent.

Of course, your ultimate aim must be to arrange a mirrorless encounter. Thus, as soon as your biceps are bulging and you are on speaking terms, make him an offer he can't refuse. A pot-holing weekend, perhaps? But don't blame me if you have a tedious time. If Mr Muscleman spends all his time adoring himself, he'll probably turn out to be incredibly boring company.

9

Lesbian & Gay Writes

A gay acquaintance of mine used to tell me that he wanted to be the fairy on the Christmas tree. I hope he was joking. Can't say it's an idea that takes my fancy.

Not that anyone has ever tried to put me on a Christmas tree – just the occasional pedestal. That's what some people do to the so-called experts – they think you know it all and can wave a magic wand to make everything bright and beautiful. No such luck my friends. Hence, when I'm asked the question, as I often am, 'And who do agony aunts write to if they have a problem', it warms the cockles of my heart. 'Aha', I say to myself, 'here is an individual who can recognise a mere mortal when they see one.'

But I also enjoy answering the question in question. I can't, of course, talk on behalf of other agony aunts, but I can say that I'm in a very lucky position. 'Tis not every nice Jewish Sex Therapist who has her own special hotline to a wise and wonderful homosexual priest. My undying devotion to the confidant concerned and particular gratitude for further insights into the gay world. And, it's the gay world that follows. Lamentably, not as gay as it should be but we'll have to keep working for a better future.

★

My boyfriend is 40 and I am 21. This is my first gay relationship and I've not yet had anal intercourse. But my friend has had lots of relationships with other men and is very keen for us to extend our sexual repertoire. The problem is that I'm worried about AIDS and I am worried that anal intercourse will be painful. My friend thinks I am being stupid. What do you think?

You are not stupid; you are very wise. It's only natural to be fearful of an illness which, with present knowledge, is incurable. Nonetheless, you seem to be confused about how AIDS is acquired; it is *not* acquired exclusively by anal intercourse. I'd like to suggest that you contact the

Terrence Higgins Trust Helpline and discuss with them how you and your partner can extend your sexual repertoire 'safely'. Seeing that your boyfriend is so experienced, you might also like to discuss the possibility of being tested for HIV. As for anal intercourse ... it can be painful if you are not mentally ready for it and if the active partner does not have the right techniques.

★

My partner, a kind and cheerful woman of 28, has become a Jekyll and Hyde sort of person. Our relationship of the past seven years went smoothly. We loved and respected each other and sexually we were very compatible. She is now depressed most of the time and took an overdose of aspirins not long ago. Fortunately, I arrived home in time to save her. The trouble is that, since her discharge from hospital, she has started saying that I am trying to poison her and refuses to eat. I do not need to say that sex is now non-existent and I spend most of my time trying to console her during her bouts of sobbing. I am also getting depressed after these months of suffering. I love her very much and want to help her but how?

Your partner is undergoing personal trauma. It is difficult to say what has led to her present situation but what is certain, particularly after her attempted suicide, is that she needs professional help. It's easy, at the beginning, to care profoundly for someone that we love and attempt to 'rescue' them when they are ill. But, being human, we all have our breaking point. You don't need to cope on your own. In the first instance, your friend should be seen by her GP who will be able to make a suitable referral. And, by the way, as I'm sure you know, this is not the time to put any pressure on her regarding sex. Do keep me posted.

★

One year ago my 22 year old son announced to me that he was gay. I love him dearly but still can't come to terms with the fact that his other half is a man. I'm not really prejudiced in other respects but, much as I'd like to understand my son's behaviour, to me it's not normal. I don't want to think like this but I'm afraid that I will never adjust to what is going on. He is aware of my feelings and I know that he too finds the situation painful. Is this something I will have to live with or do you think that I might adjust in time?

I hope that you will adjust in time. Basically, it was a sign of your son's love and confidence in you that allowed him to 'come out'. He obviously didn't want to hurt you but was hoping to share something enriching in his life. For many parents it can be a major trauma coming to terms with the fact that they don't have total control over their childrens' lives. I, for one, fancied a career in dentistry for my eldest, thinking that she would finance my aged avocations when I eventually retire to the Costa Geriatrica. She's intending to be a piano player in a Spanish nightclub. That's the way it crumbles, offspring-wise.

But, back to your son. There is far too much judgement around regarding other peoples sexual preferences. He has plenty to cope with from a hostile society. If you are genuinely trying to understand his lifestyle, ask the London Lesbian and Gay Switchboard to refer you to a group for the parents of gay men.

★

I have come to the end of the relationship with my boyfriend. It is no longer constructive and we do nothing but bitch at each other. We keep together because doing so seems better than the pain and loneliness that will follow, but we are destroying each other. He left his job two weeks ago and when I came home from work one day, I caught him in bed having a threesome with two older men. I was furious but he laughed and told me in no uncertain terms to piss off. We own the house together and our economics are all joint. I have decided to leave him. What shall I do?

Yes, you have arrived at the end of your relationship. This man is telling you that you are no longer important in his life, yet hasn't got the guts to discuss it in a civilised way. Somehow or other, you must find a way of making a clean break and starting life afresh. If you don't, you will lose all remaining dignity and become more depressed than ever. For support, contact the London Lesbian and Gay Switchboard and Gay Legal Advice.

★

I live in a village and am one of the few young men around here. I know I am gay because I am not interested in women but I have great fantasies about the other young men I see. Lately, rumours have been going around about me being a 'poof' and the only friend I have is now totally against me and makes fun of me when he sees me in the street. I am becoming a recluse. What can I do to improve my situation?

I'm sorry to hear that you are leading such a difficult and secretive existence. Is there not a gay group that you could join, perhaps in a nearby town? I'm sure that once you find a congenial social outlet, you will become much happier and less affected by the stupid people who are taunting you. If there is no gay community nearby and your misfortunes continue, it may be worth considering a move from your village to a place in which your sexual inclinations will not be the measure of your worth.

★

I recently went on holiday and, rather rashly, had an affair with a guy I met on the plane. Stupidly, I didn't ask him anything about his sexual history and, although we used condoms, I'm now very worried that I might have caught AIDS. I'd be most grateful if you could answer my letter quickly as I'm in such a state. Thanks.

Sorry that your holiday sex is now tormenting you. Asking people about their sexual history can be difficult and is too often forgotten in the heat of the moment. But I'm pleased to hear that you did take the precaution of using condoms. To be at peace with yourself, arrange to be seen at your local Sexually Transmitted Diseases (STD) Clinic. You'll be able to talk with a counsellor and work out whether or not you wish to be tested for HIV.

★

Three nights ago, I met this guy in a bar, took him home and had sex with him. He was very pleasant and the sex was good and safe. Next day he refused to leave, saying that he was unemployed, homeless and I would enjoy having him around. But he's taken over the flat, invites people round and yesterday I caught him in bed with a really rough character. They both laughed when I shouted at them to leave immediately. The truth is that in a situation like this I am not able to be assertive and am physically incapable of throwing him out. What can I do? He has copied the front door key and comes and goes as he pleases.

I am afraid that you have become involved with a nasty piece of work who will – if nothing is done – continue to abuse you and your home. Try very firmly to show him the door; change the lock if he leaves the flat and put his possessions outside. If this fails, I don't think that you will have much alternative but to go to the police and explain the position to them. And next time around, do watch who you invite into your home. Too many over-trusting gay men have found themselves in the most awkward of situations.

★

I am now 33. All my life I have enjoyed picking up people in public toilets. I was arrested by the police three days ago and have to appear in court in two weeks' time. I am pleading guilty because I have nothing to lose. My family lives far away and everyone at work knows I am gay. Since my arrest, I feel it is about time to settle, find someone who really loves me and give up all this sex without feeling, but I torment myself thinking I will not be able to stay away from toilets. Do you have any suggestions?

Are you sure you will be able to stop 'cottaging'? The shock of arrest after so many years of 'successful unfeeling sex' may be the cause of your new thinking. But you could be in the same situation as the man with bronchitis who stops smoking until he is feeling better. I don't want to be pessimistic but 'cottaging' is addictive and you must be very strongly motivated to change your ways. If you genuinely believe that this is what you want to do, psychotherapy could help you.

★

I am a 23 year old gay with no interest whatsoever in younger men, particularly under the age of 16. Last week a note was put through my letter box unsigned. It was a threat from someone who said he was 15 and had heard of me being gay. He wanted to be invited into my house and have sex with me because he fancied me. If I did not leave a specific signal outside the door to say 'yes', he said he would go to the police and accuse me of having had sex with him. I am frightened because I did not dare to leave the signal required and he may carry out his threat. If there is a next time, should I ask him to come in and try to explain that I am not interested?

No. Do not, under any circumstances, invite this boy into your home. You will be leaving yourself open to further blackmail particularly as, if he wants to hurt you, he will be able to describe the inside of your home. Not taking any notice is the best way to avoid a 'fatal attraction' situation but, at the same time, it would be wise to be prepared for further trouble. I certainly hope that you did not throw away the note that he sent you and would suggest that you keep any further messages from him. It's possible that, if you ignore the stupid boy and his threats, you'll hear nothing further from him. But, to be on the safe side, have a word with Gay Legal Advice.

★

Please help me. I am desolate. For the past 5 years I lived with a man who meant everything to me. We had so much in common – music, love of our home, our jobs and holidays. He died three weeks ago of a heart attack. The problem is that during our relationship we were so happy with each other that we neglected our family and friends. Now I find myself totally alone and unable to contact anyone. I feel suicidal and have not left the house since his death.

I feel for you. You are going through a process of grief which is difficult to bear. Sadly, one of the disadvantages of being gay is that many people do not realise that the pain of losing someone you love is the same as for anyone else. In a happy relationship, other friendships are necessary and, although you have neglected such friendships in the past, you mustn't continue to do so. Please call your previous friends and family and tell them how you feel. I'm quite sure that some of them will rally round and do their very best to help you. And contact the London Lesbian and Gay Switchboard if you wish to be put in touch with a gay bereavement group.

★

My lover and I have been together for 7 years. He was married before and has two boys who are now 10 and 12. Our relationship with his ex-wife has been surprisingly good but there are problems now. She is getting married again and has asked us to have the children for occasional weekends and holidays. I don't think this is a good idea for obvious reasons. Should I put my foot down?

I'm concerned about your reference to 'obvious reasons'. What are the obvious reasons? The children may be happy to visit you; your boyfriend's ex-wife does not appear to have qualms and, I suspect, neither does her future husband. They presumably know and trust you. And why shouldn't they? Perhaps you are worried about the responsibility but why not give it a try? Providing that you put some thought and effort into the time spent with the boys, you will probably find that their visits enrich all of your lives.

★

I am a lesbian and have been sharing my house with a girlfriend two years younger. I have no hang-ups about my lesbianism and have adjusted

*in all respects. My lover tells me that she is not sure if she wants to continue
our relationship because her parents are insisting that she gets married and
has children. I suspect this is an excuse because she has been seeing a man
of her own age for the past six months. I thought he was just a friend but I
now suspect that the relationship is more intimate than that. Please advise.*

Your letter is full of 'I suspect'. Assuming too much, however,
can be dangerous. You really must sit down with your friend and
ask her what's happening. Does she want your relationship with her
to continue? Is she 'just good friends' with this man or are they having
an affair? Does she herself now wish to get married but is using her
parents' pressure as an excuse for you? Until you have the facts at hand,
I don't see that you can make plans for the future. Good luck and do
write again if you'd like to.

★

*I've recently 'come out' and find that I am experiencing a number of
problems which I'm sure other gays must share. Can you suggest any reading
material on the subject which might make me feel a little less isolated?*

Well, first of all, congratulations on 'coming out'. You've taken a
big step and, although you are sure to encounter difficulties along the
way, you will probably find it a most liberating experience. I'd suggest
that you subscribe to the various gay journals available like *Gay Times*,
Capital Gay and so on. Full of interesting reading and other people's
perceptions of gay life. And treat yourself to a copy of *How to be a
Happy Homosexual – A Guide for Gay Men* by Terry Sanderson. It's
down to earth and most informative.

★

*I am very confused. I feel randy and able to come but don't seem to
get a full, hard erection. As I'm always passive and don't have to penetrate
when having sex, this does not matter. But some of the people I've had sex
with were put off by my lack of hardness. Is there an operation which
will put this right?*

The mechanics of erection are different from the mechanics of
ejaculation. Thus there are men, like yourself, who are able to ejaculate
when not fully erect. It's a common problem which could be due to a
thousand different causes. There's certainly no need for you to have an
operation. I'd suggest that you arrange to see your GP for a check up

and, assuming that all is well, ask for referral to a Sex Therapist.

Regarding your passivity, I'm not convinced that gays are either active or passive (thinking about it ... no different from straights). It's more likely that they condition themselves to perform in one particular way. Once you are feeling more confident about your sexuality, you'll probably find that you could well enjoy some 'safer' sexual activity.

★

I am 92 years old and have been gay since I was 30. I work at the address below. Anyway, if you know of anybody who is about the same age, please contact me. I would be very interested. Thank you.

As you well know, dear reader, I am a professional Sex Therapist with limited free time and no inclination to run an introduction agency. But I get the feeling that a 92 year old, employed in the travel business, is going to survive with or without my help.

Nevertheless, as you've made the effort to write to me, I may as well make a suggestion or two.

Why not use your employment to your advantage and share your problem with your boss? She/he might be delighted to save on the PRESTEL bill and send you to the heavenly hotspots of Amsterdam – playground of the patriarchs. Could be ecstasy for you and will give me the opportunity to return to the serious art of agony!

★

My boyfriend and I met four years ago. We both had been pretty promiscuous and were longing for a monogamous and fulfilling relationship. When we decided to buy our house and share life, we made mutual promises of loyalty to each other. I am in no doubt that he has kept his promise to me but I am getting itchy feet. On several occasions, I have invited previous partners to the house with the intention of seducing them but stopped short at the very last minute. I would like good advice on what to do. Thank you.

You are confusing fancying other people with going the whole hog and having sex with them. Deep down, I don't get the impression that you want to be disloyal; after all, the relationship you have seems to have worked well for a long time now. Perhaps you must both review what is happening sexually between you? Is sex becoming boring? Have you 'settled' too much and are finding that the 'marital' routine is getting to you? I would confront these questions by having a heart to heart conversation with your partner. Once you are in the process of communicating your feelings to each other, you will be able to work out how to give 'sexual life' to a relationship which, in all other ways, seems to make you happy.

★

I think I need your advice. I have known I was homosexual since the age of 15 when I had my first experience with a younger boy. I am now 26 and very worried because I keep following boys of 8 and 13 in the street, although I don't go near them. All my fantasies are about boys in this age group. I tried to have sex with an older gay but it was a total disaster. Basically it made me sick. My worries are that the longings are getting stronger. I am not eating properly or sleeping properly and I am aware of the legal implications if anything ever happens. Please help me.

You sound very confused about whom you really are. You are not a homosexual but a paedophile i.e. someone who likes boys in their puberty. Real homosexuals prefer the adult to adult relationship. You are quite right to worry about the legal implications – understandably, society is very antagonistic towards paedophiliacs, and you could get into serious trouble with the law if anything untoward were to happen. Please take my advice and seek professional help quickly. I would suggest that you ask your GP for a referral to the nearest Sexual Dysfunction Clinic.

★

Two days ago, my boyfriend, with whom I have had a marvellous relationship, announced that his HIV test was positive. I will be tested shortly, and the result will not alter my feelings for my lover. However we are both highly promiscuous, always involving a third person in our love-making. I know that I will be able to stop this promiscuity but my lover says he wants us to carry on as before. How can I convince him that what we have been doing is now dangerous for others?

It may be difficult. Your boyfriend appears to be somewhat blind and selfish in his attitude. There is an epidemic out there and every one – not just the gay community – has a responsibility for not spreading it further. You have no choice but to be straightforward. Tell your boyfriend that you are no longer prepared to include a third party in your love-making and that new and safer ways of enjoying sex between the pair of you must be found. This may well create problems initially but, if the love you feel for each other is genuine, you ought to be able to resolve your problems. Good luck.

★

My boyfriend's parents don't know he's gay and living with me. He visits his parents every weekend and, of course, can't take me home with him. I get very lonely and really feel that it's about time he told his parents what's going on but he refuses to do this. Don't you think it would be better if he were to be honest with his family? Or am I being selfish? I'd really like to spend some time with my boyfriend at weekends and feel that, if his parents knew what was going on, they might eventually come to terms with our relationship and invite me to their home with my boyfriend.

Yes, you are being a little selfish and he is being a trifle thoughtless, if you don't mind me saying so! It's much more difficult for some people to 'come out' than for others and, contrary to popular advice, I don't like to recommend that someone 'come out' unless they have a good emotional, social and psychological support system. Talk with your friend and attempt to arrive at an agreement. Perhaps he could visit his parents less frequently. And could you not invite his parents to visit you, not as a gay couple, but as two friends who share a home? Once they have seen the set-up a few times, they may start asking questions and you may both be ready to be open with them.

★

I am a 35 year old gay guy and have been living with my boyfriend for seven years. Recently, he told me that he had secretly been seeing a woman and that they are planning to get married in the spring. I am devastated and feel suicidal. Please help.

You've been treated very badly and I'm not surprised that you are feeling so depressed. I can only say that your 'friend' is playing a dangerous game and will get caught out in the end. He is obviously not to be trusted and, however painful it is now, in the long term I'm sure that you'll be better off without him. Meanwhile, call the Lesbian and Gay Switchboard and ask them to put you in touch with a good supportive counsellor. And please don't give up hope. You will find that, once you have been away from your 'friend' for a while, the pain will ease and life will be happier without the confusion that he has created.

★

I am a lesbian living with another woman and her four year old son. We've been together for six months and, during this time, my mother has refused to visit. I am extremely depressed as I had such a good relationship with my mother prior to this. She knew I was a lesbian but she now feels that it's wrong that two lesbian women are bringing up a young boy. He seems perfectly happy and my partner and I are also very happy. How can I make my mother see that everything is okay? I really miss her visits.

Yes, this sort of reaction is painful for you, but sometimes we have to make a choice between parents and lovers and, at present, this seems to be the case in your life. Employ more time in loving your woman friend, make sure that her son has a good home and let your mother make her own decisions about her relationship with you. The truth is that six months is a short time to allow other people to settle around any relationship. With luck, your mother's reactions will become more positive as time goes by.

★

My boyfriend and I have been living together for four years. We have a great relationship but he won't tell his parents that he is gay and, on the rare occasions that he visits them, he always takes home a female friend who he passes off as his girlfriend. I feel very hurt and insulted by this. Do you think I should try and put a stop to it? If so, how?

I personally feel that the sort of deceit that you describe is a recipe for disaster. But, if your boyfriend insists on taking home a 'mock' girlfriend, I don't think that you can put a stop to it, just like that. What you can do is discuss your feelings with your boyfriend, as calmly as possible, and without anger and accusations. And, hard as it might be, attempt not to be too impatient. Your boyfriend may well feel ready to spill the beans at some point in the future when the time is right for him to do so.

★

Do you think I should tell my friends that my daughter is a lesbian? They are always asking me whether or not she has got a boyfriend and I make up lots of lies. I can't bring myself to tell them the truth but perhaps I should so that they'll stop asking me all these questions.

This is a question that I am frequently asked.
It seems to me that you really need to examine your relationship

with your daughter and work out why, deep down, you are feeling so ashamed. Regarding your friends, it's nobody's business whether your daughter is a lesbian or librarian. If you cannot tell the truth, best to remember the old Italian proverb – 'A closed mouth catches no flies' and remain silent.

★

I'm 30, gay and not in a relationship. I've got a close male friend who I really fancy in a big way but I feel quite confused by the way he acts towards me. He can be very affectionate but this display of warmth only ever surfaces when he's had too much to drink. When he is sober he is very macho and always flirting with the secretaries at work (he and I work together). I don't think that I can cope with this for much longer ... particularly as, deep down, I think he is attracted to me. What should I do?

It sounds to me as if your friend is quite confused about relating to people in general, as well as to you specifically. Sure, it's possible that he is attracted to you. It's also possible that he sees you as a good friend but, like many men, needs a drink or two before he can express emotion. You have the choice of leaving the situation as it is or confronting your friend with the fact that you are attracted to him but bewildered by his mood changes. Bear in mind that, if you do declare your feelings, he may not respond positively to them. Sadly, we don't always get what we want but that shouldn't stop us from having a go!

★

Please help. I'm female and have been in love with a girl at college for two years. I'm sure she felt the same. A year ago we both went to different colleges. I'm totally obsessed by her and can't stop thinking about her. I've never felt this way before, it's scary. I know her address but I don't know if I ought to write to her. I have to do something. Tell it to me straight. What should I do for the best?

It can be an extremely confusing and painful situation when you find yourself infatuated with someone, be it of the same or opposite sex. By all means, write to this girl, if you want to do so, but I'd advise you to play it gently and not declare your true feelings at this stage. You also need to accept that she might not have felt the same about you and there is a strong possibility that she will not acknowledge your letter. In order to be able to cope with her response, one way or the other, try to reap the benefits of attending a new college. Take this opportunity to make friends, extend your interests and lead as full a life as you can.

★

I am female and I know there are other females who fancy me but I don't know how to go about getting to know them. Maybe it's because I'm scared of rejection. What can I do? I don't know of any clubs I can go to. I was chatted up by a girl I met at a party who said she fancied me but she was under the influence of alcohol and, anyway, she was an old friend and I didn't fancy her. I'm straight looking but I was worried that she might have realised that I was gay. It's all so weird. Help.

Most people are scared of rejection and those that aren't tend to be a little on the insensitive side – you are not alone in feeling this way. But, in other respects, you do strike me as being very much alone, worried that people might think you are a lesbian, yet wanting to develop an intimate friendship with another woman. There are many venues for lesbians to meet. There are also counsellors with whom you can talk through your confusions. Ring the London Lesbian and Gay Switchboard for information on both matters.

10

Mid-Life and Later

Does life begin at forty? I decided to ask this very question to a number of my comrades who have passed this significant figure. Read on for their responses.

Layla: No. It begins at 44.

Ivor: How can you expect me to answer that? Parenthood and philosophy are not compatible. I never get time to be with my brain. My future is behind me.

Manjula: Absolutely. Life is deeper, more intense. Saw the most amazing Tom Stoppard play last night. Would never have appreciated it years ago. You must stop writing this book and take the night off to see it, Sandra. Give yourself a break. You look 101.

Rosemary: There's the realisation that life is finite. Intellectually, you've always known this, but not quite believed it. Urgency can create challenge.

Fred the milkman:

    By God it does and, by the way, when are you going to pay the milk bill?

Time stops for no man, woman or beast. So here's mid-life and later, whether you like it or not.

★

I am a 55 year old male. My problem is that I am feeling rather exhausted lately because my girlfriend, who is 29, has a heavy sexual appetite. We make love at least twice a night but she still demands more sexual antics.

Do you think I'm being selfish or should I say no? I'm no spring chicken any longer. I love her very much and I do not want to hurt her feelings.

Look, if your girlfriend had wanted a spring chicken, she wouldn't be with you now. She obviously finds you very tasty and so she should. As my grandmother always used to say – 'Older chickens make better soup!' So, have a chat with your girlfriend and tell her honestly that you are tired, though not weary of her. I'm sure she'll understand what you are saying and will want to reach a compromise. Perhaps you can pleasure her in other ways without always aiming for penetration. You are not being selfish and I doubt that you'll hurt her feelings if you approach the subject with tact and love.

★

My wife, who is 50, suffers from bad arthritis of the hip. Up until a year ago we had a reasonably active sex life but lately things have not been too good. She says that she still feels sexy but finds love-making uncomfortable. Do you have any ideas?

Have you been making love in the missionary position? I ask this question because, very often, this position can cause considerable discomfort to women with hip problems. If so, it could be that a change to another position might prove to be more comfortable for your wife. Why don't you experiment and see what suits her best?

I also think you'd find it worthwhile contacting SPOD, the association to aid the sexual and personal relationships of people with a disability. Ask for their information sheets on sex and arthritis.

★

Over the last few years, I've noticed that, once I've had an erection, I can't get another one for a long time afterwards. Is this unusual? Do I have a problem? I'm in my 50s.

It's in no way unusual and the only problem you have is that you are probably comparing your sexual functioning to the way it was in previous decades. Sexual changes do occur as we age. It's often the case that it takes longer to achieve the first erection and that, after ejaculation, it could take anything up to 24 hours before a chap can become erect again. Some men find that their penises are not as full or as hard as they once were. Others discover that it can take longer to ejaculate and that their ejaculatory force ain't what it used to be. But can

I say loud and clear that none of this means you can't enjoy a fulfilling sex life. What's more, some of this means that it could be even more fulfilling than ever.

★

What exactly is hormone replacement therapy? My doctor has suggested that I have a course of treatment but I don't know whether to or not.

Hormone replacement therapy is the name for a course of the female hormones, oestrogen and progestogen. The aim in increasing the supply of hormones at the time of the menopause and afterwards is to reduce or postpone some of the uncomfortable physical effects, experienced by many women at this stage of their life. Some women have found HRT enormously beneficial. Others have complained of severe side-effects. I cannot say whether or not this form of treatment will suit you but can only suggest that you return to your GP for a detailed discussion on the pros and cons, before deciding for yourself.

★

I had a prostate operation a while back. My wife and I have resumed our sex life but, when I come, nothing comes out! What's happening?

A prostatectomy tends not to affect other aspects of sexual functioning but may impair the capacity to ejaculate or lead to the 'dry' orgasm, which is what you are experiencing. What's happening is that you are not ejaculating via normal channels, so to speak. Instead, the ejaculate is going into your bladder. Sounds odd, I know, but it's all perfectly normal and nothing to worry about. There is no reason as to why your sexual pleasure should not be as great as it was prior to the operation.

★

Just writing to say that my wife and I are both 73. We have a very good sex life and always enjoy reading your column.

Well, I am delighted to hear that you enjoy both the column and your sex life. It's always nice to hear from satisfied customers!

★

My husband has suddenly moved into the spare room without telling me why. I don't understand it. We've had a long and successful marriage and a satisfying sex life. Do you think he could be having an affair with someone else? How can I make him talk?

Does your husband normally deal with conflict by withdrawing? Despite what you say about your relationship in the past, I suspect he's never been very good at confronting problems directly but prefers to step side-ways like a crab. When he steps into the spare room, however, you have no alternative but to insist he tells you what's going on. He is experiencing a crisis of some sort and you need to know what it is. Ask him outright; tell him you cannot live in impenetrable silence and want to hear the whole truth, distressing though it may be. I wish you luck. Do let me know how you get on.

★

I am very fed up with the way that people react to me, men in particular. I am a 46 year old woman, recently divorced, and I feel that every man I meet treats me like a mother. Do you think that I should stop looking for another partner? It seems to me that all the men I know who are available are looking for someone young and beautiful and I'm beginning to feel that I've had it. Do you agree?

No, I don't agree that you've had it. Neither do I agree that *all* men are on the look out for a young and beautiful companion — just some of them! So, where do we go from here? My feeling is that, since you are only recently divorced, now is not the time to go all out in search of a new partner. Liaisons formed on the rebound are often disasters. Play it cool. Give yourself time to get to know some men as friends, rather than eyeing them up as potential husbands. That way, you stand a much better chance of forming a rewarding and long-lasting relationship. And you'll avoid the danger of rushing into an unsatisfactory situation simply because you feel you must have a man in tow in order to be a complete person.

★

My husband and I are both sixty and still make love regularly. Do you think that this is normal? Should we both be slowing down?

Although our sexual desires and capabilities tend to change as we age, there is no reason whatsoever for them to disappear. The urge and capacity to make love can continue into advanced old age.

There are certainly no rules and regulations regarding how often anyone, at any given stage in their life, should make love. In your case, you are obviously doing what's normal for you and that's what matters. And should you be slowing down? Not unless you want to.

★

I am a 65 year old woman. I have been married for many years but I have only had sex three times. I have always found it disgusting and have encouraged my husband to find other women. My husband and I are still together and he would still like to have sex with me. Do you think there is any point in seeking help with this problem or have we left it too late?

It's not easy to change the habits of a lifetime but I don't think that it can ever be too late to seek help, if you genuinely want to improve your situation. I often see people of your age in my sex therapy practice and although I cannot pretend that everyone benefits from seeking professional help, it's clear that many do and that changes, however late in the day, can occur. Why don't you write to the Association of Sexual and Marital Therapists or visit your GP who may be able to refer you to an appropriate therapist.

★

I am 62 and recently met a woman near my age. She is very exciting but I cannot hold an erection. I am taking blood pressure reducing pills. Do you think this has any bearing on my problem and should I stop taking them?

Certain drugs, prescribed to lower blood pressure, can interfere with sexual response and it's possible that an adjustment of dosage or change of drug may help to resolve your problem. I do not think that you should stop taking the tablets without first seeking a medical opinion and would recommend that you discuss this matter with your GP. But it's also possible that, as a result of entering into a new relationship, you are a little nervous and worrying unduly about your sexual performance. If this is the case, you might be well advised to share your anxieties with your new woman friend. She'll understand, if she cares about you and you'll probably begin to relax.

★

My wife and I are both in our 40s and our sex life has become monotonous. Do you think we are too old to change our ways and make our love-making more lively?

Well, you are hardly very old but, even if you were, I don't believe that you can't teach old dogs new tricks, providing that the dogs want to learn them. If you are looking for inspiration, treat yourself to *Treat Yourself to Sex* by Paul Brown and Carolyn Faulder. I think you'll enjoy putting into practice some of the 'sexpieces', recommended in the book.

★

My friend told me that if I have hormone replacement therapy, for the menopause, it will make me more fertile. I am very worried about this because I don't want any more babies at my age! I'm 53.

I am happy to inform you that your friend's advice is totally inaccurate. Hormone replacement therapy (HRT) will not make you more fertile. Once you have passed the natural menopause, you won't be able to conceive, and the regular bleeding caused by certain forms of HRT won't alter this in any way.

★

My husband, over the years, has become more and more conventional and routine. We are both 57 now. Our sex life is barely alive. All he seems to do is work, eat, watch the telly and sleep. I love him but would like to be able to demonstrate my love physically. Any ideas?

Well, let's look to Newton's first law of motion for some inspiration. He concluded that 'if no force acts on a body in motion, it will continue to move uniformly in a straight line.' If you want your husband to liven up, don't leave it to him to get a move on. The time has arrived for you to get into action and be more forceful. Nothing too out of the ordinary for starters but, slowly and subtly, encourage him to toe a different line. Treat him to a night out on the town. Organise something special that you've not done for ages. He probably once wooed you. Your turn now.

★

I've always enjoyed a regular sex life with my husband but, since the menopause, I find sexual intercourse very uncomfortable. Do you have any suggestions?

After the menopause, some women do find that the vagina becomes less moist and I imagine that this is why you are finding sexual intercourse uncomfortable. A simple remedy is to use a lubricating jelly, like KY Jelly, which you can buy over the counter at any chemist. If this does not prove to be helpful, then have a word with your GP who may decide to prescribe a course of oestrogen cream.

I am 40 and have been married for 20 years. I love my wife and family. We have a very busy and active relationship except – you guessed it – our sex life. My wife never seems to have come to terms with her own sexuality or mine and will not 'relax her guard' or discuss how we could be happier. When we were first married we were young and made many mistakes, sexually. The pain of this seems to have put up barriers in her mind. For example, I love things like sexy underwear, cunnilingus etc. She thinks I am sex mad. Help!

Your wife needs to enjoy sex first before she can appreciate sexy underwear, cunnilingus etc. Go back to the beginning and woo her again. Take it at her pace with tenderness and gentle persuasion. Are you affectionate towards her when you are not having sex? If not, start being so now and you will find that it does make a difference. If you cannot sort out these problems but, in other respects, have a good life together, it would be worthwhile consulting a Sex Therapist who would be able to help you. Good luck.

★

I'm a 44 year old married woman. I always used to enjoy sex but, over the last six months, I seem to have lost my sex drive completely. A friend of mine told me that this happened to her and that the doctor gave her injections of male hormones which did the trick. Can this be true?

I understand that, very occasionally, women have been injected with male hormones in order to improve a flagging sex drive. But I must say that I have never met a doctor who has prescribed this form of treatment. In the main, loss of interest in sex is due to emotional causes. By all means, ask your GP for a physical check up to ensure that all is well. Then, if you do decide to examine your sexual problems further, I would suggest that you consult a sex therapist.

★

I am a man of 69 and am planning to marry a younger woman. We would very much like to have a baby. Do you think I am still capable of fathering a child?

Dr David Delvin, in his book *The She Complete Guide to Sex and Loving*, refers to the case of one Thomas Parr, an Elizabethan philanderer, who managed to get a young lady pregnant when he was 104 no less! So, in answer to your question, yes. If you are still capable of having sex, as I'm sure you are, then there's a good chance that you are still capable of fathering a child.

★

My mother died four months ago after a long illness. Although the rest of the family is coming to terms with her death which was expected, my father is wandering around in a terrible state. He acts as if my mother is still with us and sometimes even talks to her. Is there anything I can do to help him as his behaviour is a great worry to us all?

Being unable to accept the loss of a loved one is one of the recognisable stages of bereavement. Your father seems to be denying the fact that death has occurred which is a perfectly understandable reaction to the pain that he is experiencing. I think that you must allow your father the time to grieve, as well as making sure that he is aware that he has the support of you and the family. Once his pain begins to ease, you might be able to help him renew some of his interests.

★

I've been very happily married for years and years to a wonderful woman and we have a great sex life. But I have got a problem. I've developed a fatal fascination for our au pair girl. She's dead sexy and, even if it's pouring with rain, she wanders around in a skimpy T-shirt and Bermuda shorts. I can't take my eyes off her. I even think that she might fancy me. What am I going to do?

Nothing, if you've got any sense and value your marriage. Or, on second thoughts, if you feel you cannot resist temptation, you might do well to come up with some reason for transferring this temptress to another family. Seems to me that your marriage is more than satisfactory and it would be extremely short-sighted of you to indulge in a voyage which, at the very least, will rock the marital boat, if not cause it to capsize completely.

★

I am middle-aged and the mother of two teenage children. I have brought them up on my own, as well as working and doing everything else, and feel that, given the circumstances, I've done a reasonable job. The problem is my mother. She's always coming round to see me, criticises everything I do and points out where I am going wrong. I can't take it anymore and feel really depressed. Any advice?

I think you should tell your mother that you find her comments depressing and ask her not to be so negative when she visits. I'm sure she's aware of the struggle you've had to do the best for your children, despite your difficulties. But, like most mothers/grandmothers she probably wishes that things were different and that you hadn't had such a tough time. I guess that her concern shows itself by finding fault, instead of by more positive means. Tell her that, while you appreciate her interest, you would also appreciate her being a bit less critical.

★

I had a very difficult marriage which came to an end one year ago. My husband was an aggressive and violent man and I know that I am better off without him. The problem is that I am very depressed and still miss him even though our marriage was so bad. Please help because I don't know how to face the future alone. I am 47 with a 10 year old daughter who is living with me.

I'm glad you had the courage and fortitude to leave your husband. No-one should have to put up with violence, and you're infinitely better off without him. I know you must be lonely and that life with a 10 year old is a struggle but I think that you miss some company, as opposed to the company of your husband. Going back to him just because you are feeling lonesome would not be a good move.

What you need immediately is support, companionship and understanding and you'll find this from people in a similar situation to yourself. Why don't you contact Gingerbread which is an association for single parent families. Ask to be put in touch with a local group and try to attend some of their meetings.

★

My wife is 45 and I am 50. Although we used to have intercourse more often, we now make love about once a week. Neither of us wants sex more

*often. We like it when it happens. I don't usually discuss this sort of thing
with friends but I did mention it to a mate of mine last week. He said that
having sex once a week was well below the national average and that my
wife and I must have sexual problems. Do you think he's right?*

As your friend inspired you to write to me, you are obviously
concerned that he might be right. But of course he isn't. Some
people have sex every day. Some live without it altogether. So what!
You and your wife are presumably doing what suits you both. Coital
frequency often decreases with age but if the quality is fine, why worry
about the quantity?

★

*My husband died 18 months ago and, ever since then, I've felt deeply
depressed and don't feel that life is worth living. I am 53 and have two
grown up children who I don't often see. I don't work and feel that it's too
late to get a job now and I can't see any purpose in anything. I can't cope
with the constant loneliness that I feel but don't know how to change things.
My whole life revolved around my husband and I feel that I have died with
him. Please help.*

Grief is a slow process and it takes time to come to terms with the loss
of someone so close. I think you would find it helpful to talk through
your feelings and suggest you contact CRUSE, an organisation which
offers bereavement counselling.

It's not too late for work. If it's difficult to find paid employment,
then there are many voluntary organisations who would be delighted
to have your help, even for a few hours a week e.g. Citizens Advice
Bureaux, Age Concern, Oxfam. This would give you the opportunity
to meet other people and help to build up your self-confidence.

Finally, if there was ever something you always wanted to do and
couldn't because of your family commitments, then do it now. Whether
it be travel, studying, or a particular hobby or activity, investigate the
possibilities and put a plan into action. It's never too late. As you
become more involved in life you will find your loss easier to bear.

★

*My wife is a bit like my car. She can't get started in the mornings. That's
the time I like having sex best. We do it a lot at night but, if we could do
it in the mornings, I'd start the day much happier. How can I change her?
She's 46 and I'm a few years younger.*

Maybe you've given her too much choke and flooded her engine. You could try turning off at night and see if it alters her waking pattern. Or you may just have to come to accept that, unlike yourself, she is unable to respond sexually at the crack of dawn. If tempting her with breakfast in bed doesn't appear to be the solution, perhaps you could settle for the occasional Sunday lunch-time treat!

11

Candidly Condoms

I received a letter a while back from a chap who'd had two wives, several live-in lovers and one vasectomy. He told me that his penis felt put out of joint by the constant use of a condom.

'I hate the awful things,' he said in his letter. 'I had a vasectomy, thinking I would be a free man for ever, but it's back to square one. My latest girlfriend is petrified of AIDS and won't entertain the idea of sex unless I use this form of protection. It seems unnatural to me. What am I going to do?'

Well, Mr Vasectomy, I don't suppose it's 'natural' to wear anything anywhere but we must adapt to the weather conditions, must we not? No-one could have predicted that the condom would become the garb of the fashionable and health conscious man. But it has, so it's positive thinking for one and all.

'Better latex than never,' as somebody once said.

Carry on condoms (or mod cons, as I like to call them).

★

My boyfriend and I wish to have sex but we still have difficulties in using a condom. Can one buy condoms in different sizes and are there any instructions with them? Also is it true that they come in different flavours? Are they reusable and how do they cope in the tumble dryer?

It's not difficult to learn how to use a condom properly. They do come with instructions but, if you want further information, ring the Family Planning Information Service. Rumour has it that in the USA you can buy 3 sizes, large, extra-large and giant, but in this country most condoms are of standard size! One or two brands, developed with the AIDS virus in mind, are bigger and stronger, but the average condom does stretch to amazing proportions. They do come in different flavours. No, they are not reusable so, unless you are planning to make a condom collection for posterity, there would be little point in trying them out in the tumble dryer.

Can you recommend a condom for anal sex?

You are posing a difficult question. Whilst there have been a lot of claims about a lot of condoms, it's important to remember that condoms were originally designed with vaginal sex in mind. There is no real proof that thicker condoms are better for anal sex, although researchers are working on this subject at the moment. One can only assume, meanwhile, that, as anal sex tends to cause more friction than vaginal sex, it would be 'safer' to use a stronger condom. Ring the London Lesbian and Gay Switchboard if you want the names of particular brands.

I recently came off the pill and my boyfriend agreed that he would use a sheath. But, instead of buying normal sheaths from the chemist, he came round last night with some strange looking objects which he purchased in a sex shop. They look like condoms but they have odd things sticking out of them. He says they are safe to use as contraceptives but I'm not sure. Please advise.

Well, you were right to be cautious. Sounds to me like your boyfriend purchased some 'tickly condoms'. These are sheaths which have been designed with projections in order to give the woman extra thrills during sexual intercourse. Whether or not such thrills occur is debatable but what's certain is that such condoms are not effective as contraceptives. So, if it's contraception that you want, you'd better send your boyfriend shopping again.

My boyfriend and I started making love three months ago. He always uses a condom but I am not sure whether he knows what he is doing. After we have sex, he always leaves his penis inside me for a long time. He says that he likes the sensation but I'm scared I could get pregnant. Please advise.

Condoms can only work as a form of contraception if they are used properly and, I'm afraid to say that your boyfriend is taking risks. So, tell him from me that it's essential that he withdraws his penis before he loses his erection, making sure that he holds the condom firmly in position at the base of the penis. If he is not prepared to do this, leakage may occur and you could, as you fear, be risking pregnancy.

★

I'm gay and I have a new boyfriend who won't use a condom. He says he can't because he's circumcised. Is this true? We've only had anal sex once.

Anal sex carries a high risk of infection and it is particularly risky to indulge in this form of sex without taking 'safer sex' precautions. All men can use a condom – be they circumcised or not. Your boyfriend's attitude is irresponsible and one that you must discourage if you value your own sexual health.

★

What's the shelf life of a condom? My girlfriend and I have just split up. Should I throw my condoms away or put them aside for a sunny day?

All reputable brands of condoms carry an expiry date on the pack so read your pack and all will become clear. Most condoms tend to last for five years. By all means, put your condoms away for a sunny day if that's what you want to do, but you might decide that it would be more romantic to start a new relationship with a new set of sheaths!

★

My boyfriend and I make love every weekend when he comes home. He is away during the week on business. To be on the safe side we always use two condoms at the same time. Is there anything wrong with this and is it harmful in any way? I mustn't get pregnant.

There is nothing wrong or harmful in using two condoms at the same time but it's not necessary to do so. One condom, correctly used, should be a reliable form of contraception.

★

I want my boyfriend to use a condom but I'm scared that if I bring up the subject, he might think that I think that he's unclean. What should I do?

Suggesting that your boyfriend use a condom shows common sense and a responsible attitude and I doubt that your boyfriend will take your suggestion as a sign that you are unhappy with his state of cleanliness. He might well be relieved that you've raised the subject. Lots of men, as well as women, feel uneasy about discussing such matters. So, be bold; tell your boyfriend in a simple but direct fashion that you would like him to use a sheath. And, if you want any further information, write to the Family Planning Information Service for some of their condom leaflets.

★

My girlfriend and I always use a condom when we make love. One small problem. She's into wearing elaborate jewellery and I'm scared that she might tear the condom by accident. Could this happen? Also could you tell me if there are any side effects related to the use of the condom? Thanks very much.

Condoms tend to be fairly strong but they do occasionally get ripped by rings or long fingernails. So, suggest to your girlfriend that she bares her hands, in addition to the rest of her, when you make love! Better to be safe than sorry. And no, the use of a condom has no side effects, except in very rare cases of allergy.

★

What's happened to the musical condom?

As far as I know, the condom with the musical micro-chip at the tip, can still be purchased in Japan. The last I heard was that it's repertoire was still confined to The Beatles, although someone did say they were thinking about marketing a new version with 'He'll be coming round the mountains when he comes ...' But, be warned, my friend. If you do journey to Japan for a shopping expedition remember that such condoms do not carry the BSI Kitemark – our very own British seal of approval. When it comes to the crunch, think patriotically, buy BSI and select your own background music. Personally, I wouldn't be averse to a touch of Dire Straits but I'm only suggesting you take my advice re condoms.

I am totally confused. There are so many different brands of condoms on the market. How can I choose which one to buy?

The range of condoms on the market does seem to get wider by the day and I can certainly understand your confusion. I can't really recommend a particular brand of condom ... you'll have to choose whatever type appeals to you. What I can say is that it's essential to buy a brand marked with the British Standards Institute 'kitemark', which is an independent guarantee of quality.

★

I am male, nearly 23 and still a virgin. I see a lot of stories on TV and the like about girls getting pregnant by accident. As a virgin, there's something I don't know. If I use a condom, what are the chances of a girl getting pregnant? Are 'mistakes' usually due to the man not wearing a condom? I am worried that, even by wearing a condom, there still may be a good chance that the girl will get pregnant.

No method of contraception is 100% effective, although the experts do tell us that the combined pill, if taken properly, has a failure rate of less then 1%. The condom, with careful use, is considered to be 85-98% effective. 'Mistakes' are obviously made if unprotected sex takes place. 'Mistakes' are also made when condom users do not pay attention to the few simple guide-lines you can read on any condom packet. 'Mistakes' can occur because, very rarely, condoms can split or slip off the penis. You are being very responsible in studying the pros and cons. Ring the

Family Planning Information Service if you want further info.

★

I have been using condoms for some 18 months now but have experienced a high rate of condom failure (about 1 in 4). Surely this can't be right – I was lead to believe that condoms were a reliable method of contraception. Is this a typical failure or am I using them incorrectly?

This doesn't sound right to me. Sure, the very occasional condom doesn't do its job properly, but a failure rate of 1 in 4 is, without doubt, over the top. What are you doing with your condoms? Are you putting them on the appropriate organ? If so, are you following the instructions properly? Obviously I have no idea whether or not you are a correct condom user. I can only suggest that you stick with those condoms Kitemarked with the BSI seal of approval and that you re-read your condom leaflets.

★

I am going out with this guy and we had sex one night. I am 18 and was a virgin so I wasn't on the pill. I don't know if he wore a sheath and I am worried that I could get pregnant. I would like to go on the pill now but don't know how to go about it. Could you please advise me as I am very confused.

A sheath (condom) is a thin rubber bag which a man places on his erect penis before having intercourse. When he ejaculates, the semen is deposited in the bag rather than being released into the vagina. Had your boyfriend worn a sheath, I think you would have noticed.

One act of unprotected intercourse may lead to pregnancy. Visit your GP immediately and explain what has happened. She/he may, on this occasion, be able to prescribe morning-after contraception. And tell your GP that you would like to go on the pill. Alternatively, contact your local Family Planning Clinic – address and phone number in the phone book.

★

When my boyfriend uses a condom he likes to cover it with cooking oil because he says he likes the slippery feeling. Is this alright?

No! All lubricants used with condoms should be water based. Grease based lubricants, like cooking oil, rapidly damage the rubber of the condoms so that it stops offering protection. So tell your boyfriend to put the cooking oil back in the kitchen where it belongs and ask him to invest in a water based lubricant like 1-2-1 or KY Jelly, available at any chemist.

★

Because my girlfriend and I are unemployed we have a lot of free time in which to make love and I find that I am spending a fortune on condoms! Is it true that you can get them free of charge?

Yes. Free supplies of condoms are available from your local Family Planning Clinic. All you need to do is look up the number of your local clinic in the Phone Book and ring for an appointment.

★

My boyfriend is very reluctant to us a condom and doesn't want me to use any other form of birth control. He doesn't want me to have a baby but he says that he thinks contraception ruins the sexual act. Do you think I should still go out with him?

By all means, go out with him if that's what you want to do. But don't have sex with him unless he decides to grow up and adopt a more responsible approach towards contraception.

★

Can you use a condom more than once?

Certainly not! Condoms should only be used once, after which you should wrap them in a little toilet paper and flush them down the loo. I mention this because, if you don't wrap 'em up, they won't go down.

★

I've never used a condom before but my new girlfriend says that she won't have sex with me unless I'm prepared to do so. I'm not very happy about the idea as I've heard a lot of people say that sex with a condom is like washing your feet with your socks on. What do you think?

I think your girlfriend is being eminently sensible and you should listen to her rather than the 'lots of other people' to whom you refer.

Modern condoms are extremely sheer and the loss of feeling is so slight that it's hardly noticeable. So, why not try them out ... if you fancy, have a practice run on your own, before getting into action with your girlfriend.

★

I've read about the female condom. Where can I buy it?

The female condom consists of a polyurethane bag which the woman inserts into her vagina. It is said to prevent pregnancy and reduce the risk of sexually transmitted disease but we have no clear information as to how effective it is. Trials are currently being carried out in the UK as well as abroad but, in answer to your question, it is not yet available for purchase in this country.

★

I am the mother of three children, two boys and a girl. They are all teenagers and, from what they tell me, are sexually active. I have always prided myself in being liberal with them and able to talk about sexual matters. When they go to parties, discos etc, I always make sure they have some condoms with them ... you never know. My eldest son aged 19 had a furious row with me the other day. He said that I was trying to interfere in his life and that he is old enough to be responsible. This has hurt me deeply. Please advise.

Perhaps you are so afraid of the consequences of your children getting involved in 'unsafe sex' that you are becoming a bit of a condom tyrant. If you have discussed with them the wisdom of 'safer sex', not only in relation to AIDS and sexually transmitted diseases but also to pregnancy, then maybe it would be advisable to leave it at that. Try not to be too hurt about the argument with your son. I guess he was just trying to tell you that he's a big boy now and well prepared to deal with his own life. If this is the case, then pat yourself on the back and get on with yours.

★

I am 18, still a virgin and ashamed of it. All my mates have had sex and I don't seem able to seduce any of the girls I mix with. I even go to the extent of reassuring them and saying that, if they are scared of anything, I have condoms with me all the time. Do you have any advice?

Sure. First of all you've got to realise that a lot of people are or once were 18 year old virgins. It's a perfectly healthy condition and nothing to be ashamed of. Secondly, bear in mind that there's no point in issuing sexual invitations to the girls you meet by waving a packet of condoms in their faces. As I've said countless times before, despite the fact that I'm a Sex Therapist, I strongly believe that there's more to a relationship than sex alone. Please try and strike up some friendships with the girls you meet and save your body for that special woman with whom you will, one day, develop a loving liaison.

★

I know my wife has started an affair with a much younger man two doors away from us. I have no evidence of this but she is very kind to him and has invited him into our home (always when I am there). Since all this began, I have started to wear a condom during sex and she is suspicious of this and keeps asking why I am doing it when we have nothing to worry about. What do I do now?

You say that you have no evidence of your wife's affair with this young man. She only invites him into your home when you are present. Why can't you believe that she's made a new friend and nothing more? Is it not possible that you are tormenting yourself unnecessarily? What worries me most about your letter is that you have been incapable of discussing your anxieties with your wife, and she with you. You have suspicions of infidelity. She cannot understand your sudden use of condoms. Only by talking openly and honestly will you rid yourselves of the confusions you both appear to be experiencing.

★

My husband and I, for some strange reason, have enjoyed many a time the use of condoms during our love-making. I like sucking him with a condom on, and until now we have not given this activity any importance because, in the long run, it enhanced our sex lives. I am now feeling very guilty about using condoms because of the tremendous publicity they are getting and the subject they relate to, which disgusts me. My guilt is causing emotional problems and our love-making is suffering. Can you advise?

Sexual activity between partners which does not harm physically or emotionally and to which both partners agree, is very positive. The use of condoms, therefore, to enhance your sex life is excellent. I'm sorry you feel disgusted with recent publicity. You don't say whether this 'disgust' relates to AIDS but I suppose it must do. Perhaps you are one of the people who link this awful disease with the gay community and want to disassociate yourself from the gay world and its practices. You must be logical, however, and understand that AIDS is not exclusively a gay problem. Relax in the thought that your relationship is safe and throw that guilt out of the window.

★

I've got a real problem with condoms. I've only started using them recently but, every time I try and put one on, I lose my erection. My girlfriend has been very patient but I'm beginning to feel a real idiot. Please help.

If you are accustomed to having sex 'in the nude', so to speak, the introduction of condoms can cause a few hiccups initially.

But not to worry. Ask your girlfriend to lend a hand and help you put on the condom. If she is able to do this as part of love-making, I'm sure you won't feel so down.

Useful Addresses and Telephone Numbers

Alcoholics Anonymous
PO Box 1
Stonebow House
Stonebow
York YO1 2NJ
Telephone: 0904 644026/7/8/9

Al-Anon
61 Great Dover Street
London SE1
Telephone: 01 403 0888

Association of Sexual and Marital Therapists
PO Box 62
Sheffield S10 3TS

The Beaumont Society
BM Box 3084
London WC1N 3XX

Brook Advisory Centres
Head Office
153A East Street
London SE17 2SD
Telephone: 01 708 1234

CRUSE
The National Organisation for the Widowed and their Children
126 Sheen Road
Richmond
Telephone: 01 940 4818/9047

The Family Planning Information Service
27-35 Mortimer Street
London W1N 7RJ
Telephone: 01 636 7866

Gamblers Anonymous
17/23 Blantyre Street
London SW10 0DT:
Telephone: 01 352 3060 (24 hour service)

Gingerbread
35 Wellington Street
London WC2E 7BN
Telephone: 01 240 0953

GLLAD (Gay and Lesbian Legal Advice)
Telephone: 01 253 2043 (Tues-Fri 7-10pm)

Identity Counselling Service
Beauchamp Lodge
2 Warwick Crescent
London W2 6NE
Telephone: 01 289 6175

London Lesbian and Gay Switchboard
BM Switchboard
London WC1N 3XX
Telephone: 01 837 7324 (24 hour service)

London Rape Crisis Centre (for women and young girls)
PO Box 69
London WC1X 9NJ
Telephone: 01 278 3956 (office hours)
01 837 1600 (24 hour service)

Narcotics Anonymous
PO Box 417
London SW1O 0RN
Telephone: 01 351 6794 (2-8pm)
1 351 6066 for recorded list of meetings

RELATE (formerly Marriage Guidance Council)
Herbert Grey College
Little Church Street
Rugby
Warwickshire
Telephone: Rugby (0788) 565675

The Samaritans
17 Uxbridge Road
Slough
Berkshire SL1 8SN
Telephone: Slough (0753) 32713

SCODA (Standing Conference on Drug Abuse)
1-4 Hatton Place
London EC1N 8ND
Telephone: 01 430 2341

SPOD (The Association to Aid the Sexual and Personal Relationships
of People with a Disability)
286 Camden Road
London N7 0BJ
Telephone: 01 607 8851/2

The Terrence Higgins Trust
BM AIDS
London WC1N 3XX
Helpline: 01 242 1010 (3-10pm daily)

Women's Health and Reproductive Rights Information Centre
52-54 Featherstone Street
London EC1Y 8RT
Telephone: 01 251 6332/6580